Things in Every Room

Things in Every Room

HELEN LONGSTRETH

JONATHAN CAPE
LONDON

1 3 5 7 9 10 8 6 4 2

Jonathan Cape, an imprint of Vintage, is part of the
Penguin Random House group of companies

Vintage, Penguin Random House UK, One Embassy
Gardens, 8 Viaduct Gardens, London SW11 7BW

penguin.co.uk/vintage
global.penguinrandomhouse.com

First published in hardback by Jonathan Cape in 2026

Copyright © Helen Longstreth 2026

The moral right of the author has been asserted

Earlier versions of two chapters have been previously published as
'A Recipe for Forgiveness' in the *New Yorker* and
'The Green and the Gold' in the *Paris Review*.

The quoted text on p. 169 is from 'The Sound of the River'
in *The Collected Short Stories* by Jean Rhys.

The quoted text on p. 179 is from *Smile Please:
An Unfinished Autobiography* by Jean Rhys.

The quoted text on p. 181 is from *Good Morning, Midnight* by Jean Rhys.

No part of this book may be used or reproduced in any manner for the purpose
of training artificial intelligence technologies or systems. In accordance
with Article 4(3) of the DSM Directive 2019/790, Penguin Random House
expressly reserves this work from the text and data mining exception.

Set in 13.5/16.2pt Bembo Book MT Pro
Typeset by Six Red Marbles UK, Thetford, Norfolk

Printed and bound in Great Britain by Clays Ltd, Elcograf S.p.A.

The authorised representative in the EEA is Penguin Random House
Ireland, Morrison Chambers, 32 Nassau Street, Dublin D02 YH68

A CIP catalogue record for this book is available from the British Library

ISBN 9781787335295

Penguin Random House is committed to a sustainable future
for our business, our readers and our planet. This book is made
from Forest Stewardship Council® certified paper.

For my mother

'Safe, safe, safe,' the heart of the house beats proudly. 'Long years —' he sighs. 'Again you found me.' 'Here,' she murmurs, 'sleeping; in the garden reading; laughing, rolling apples in the loft. Here we left our treasure —' Stooping, their light lifts the lids upon my eyes. 'Safe! safe! safe!' the pulse of the house beats wildly. Waking, I cry, 'Oh, is this your buried treasure? The light in the heart.'

>Virginia Woolf, *A Haunted House*

PART ONE
Behind a Closed Door

Frank

When I think about my father he is standing in the kitchen gazing into space. On the counter are all the ingredients for dinner, chopped and ready in neat piles. A cookbook is propped on its stand. His white hair is combed neatly to the side, and he's wearing a brown-and-white checkered shirt tucked into a pair of wrinkled beige chinos. He has on ribbed socks and worn blue slippers because he hasn't left the house all day. He turns to me and says, 'Hi, sweetheart.' His sad eyes are magnified by his round glasses but he smiles slightly. Then he sighs, picks up his book and waits. Soon my mother will be home.

He told me once that he didn't remember his parents talking at the dinner table. He then joked that he didn't remember his parents talking at all. He grew up in 1950s Hudson, Ohio. His father was a brash and charismatic Latin teacher and track coach at the prep school across the road from their house. His mother was a smart and unhappy housewife. For dinner she would prepare things like sliced beef with boiled vegetables or spaghetti sauce over bread with iceberg lettuce, and they'd eat to the sound of the five o'clock news. Then, even if it was still light out, his mother would go to bed with a secret bottle of sherry and his father would leave to spend the rest of the night at the local bar.

Whenever my grandmother did use a recipe, maybe for a birthday cake or a barbecue, it would have been from *The Joy of Cooking*. My dad had his own copy of the hefty thousand-page book which still sits on the kitchen shelf of my childhood home, gathering dust between cookbooks by Claudia Roden and Marcella Hazan. The once white cover is now stained and tattered, the word *Joy* standing out in cheerful letters along the spine.

There are hundreds of pages in my dad's copy that have never been touched. Recipes and instructions that speak of another age: a chapter on dinner-party etiquette, a fruit salad with mayonnaise, an illustrated two-page spread on how to skin a squirrel or boil a porcupine. But other pages are splattered from decades of use. Recipes for peanut butter cookies, floating island, the roast ham we always had on Boxing Day. There are his own additions, symbolic of his life in England, where he moved in 1973: notes translating Fahrenheit to Celsius, a folded *Guardian* clipping of Felicity Cloake's 'How to Make Perfect Pumpkin Pie' from October 2010. Dishes that gave his British children a taste of their heritage and brought back America when he missed it.

He discovered his love of cooking during his third

year at Harvard in 1969, after he moved into a co-op of twenty-four people who each took a turn making dinner for the whole group. The budget was tight, and it was an all-day affair to get everything ready by six fifteen p.m., but he and his classmates found a new kind of eating culture at this communal table, far from the TV dinners and canned soups of their childhoods. Each night, they lingered over long, imaginative meals, the result of every cook trying to outdo the last. I can picture my father – a bright, cool and competitive social studies major – sat at the edge of a smoky table. He is quietly stoned and smug in steel-rimmed glasses, long curly hair and a red Maoist bandana. It is the end of the 1960s but they still believe in the revolution and the paella he spent all day cooking is going down very well.

He joined another collective house when he moved to London in 1973 to do his PhD at the London School of Economics. He and his girlfriend teamed up with three other couples and bought a wreck in Crouch End for a few thousand pounds. Over the years, the couples swapped around and the walls of the house began to buckle, quite literally. He met another LSE radical who, like him, longed for a more stable life. Within weeks he proposed; she turned him down, though they were married within the year. In 1980 he got a job teaching sociology at the University of Bath. My older brother Kimber was born the next year, followed by my sister Rachel two years later.

Perhaps it was the early years of fatherhood that threw him off-balance: squeezed by domestic life, the full-time university job, and the rise of Thatcherism, he lost faith in his research. He experienced debilitating depression and episodes of disorienting mania. He began to drink heavily for the first time, and found another escape in love affairs that he did not hide well. Seeing his family suffer, he would return to self-hatred, from which only drink offered him respite. But even during the worst times, Saturday evening would find him in the kitchen, cooking for his family to the tune of *Jazz Record Requests*.

In 1985, he picked up a book by an American novelist who'd been at Harvard at the same time he had. He asked around, soon discovering that she was now living with two young children in Oxford, my older siblings Matthew and Emma, at the tail end of a messy divorce. My dad wrote her a letter, first to say how much he'd been enjoying the snarky book reviews she'd been writing for the *Observer*, then to enquire whether she'd ever read a book she actually liked.

By his account, he was completely drunk when they met a few weeks later, at a pub across from Didcot Parkway. My mother didn't even notice. She'd grown up in Istanbul, on the campus of an American college in a bohemian community where most adults, including her Irish-American father, were hard drinkers.

It didn't take long for them to fall in love. They saw in each other another chance at life. My dad left his wife and family and moved into the cottage my mother was renting in Oxford with Matthew and Emma. He said he didn't want to have any more children. And then he said he did, before deciding again that he didn't. My mother dreamed of children who might bring their broken families together. I was born less than a year into their new life. Before I was a year old she was pregnant with my sister Pandora, and we were living midway up one of Bath's seven hills in a big dilapidated stone house on the Wellsway, owned by two Eastern Europeans who lived in the bungalow next door and received weekly shipments of furniture at odd hours.

I don't remember much about the times when we were all together under one roof. The household was frantic with noise and laughter and big fights I couldn't understand but in the middle of all that we 'little ones' were much adored. My ten-year-old sister Emma would wake up at six a.m., get dressed in her school uniform, peel me from my mother's tired arms and feed me scrambled egg. After school she and nine-year-old Rachel would dress Pandora and me up as dolls and bring us into their dance routines. Emma and thirteen-year-old Kimber would dress up as spies to inspect fourteen-year-old Matthew's room for drugs. Matthew would let me jump on his bed whenever he listened to Nirvana. The boys loved to frighten me with a rubber Frankenstein mask and then tickle me until I cried. If I came downstairs after bedtime and found them all eating dinner without me, I cried like a lion, they said.

When they had to go back to their other families, I cried even more.

Somewhere in the background, my mother was writing novels and picking up whatever newspaper work she could – but never quite enough to cover the bills. My father, by this point, was drinking beer at breakfast, turning up at work drunk, or not at all, and steadily losing his mind. The bipolar that had emerged in his thirties had sprouted wings by his forties. On the high days, he took charge of the kitchen, flying us around the world with his recipes to the soundtrack of UB40's 'Red Red Wine'. There were crazed feasts that seemed to have come from another planet, like the time he cooked six young kids an incredibly spicy clam stew followed by pumpkin pie served in a pumpkin. He spent his nights crying to *Harvest Moon* on a loop. He bullied Emma when he was drunk. He threatened Matthew. He hit his son Kimber. When I was five, he drove into a country field drunk out of his mind, attached a tube to the exhaust pipe, and tried to kill himself. He passed out and woke up two hours later, to discover the exhaust had blown the hosepipe off. Still drunk, he showed up at his ex-wife's house, sobbing in front of his children, ranting and raving about how he'd 'given it the old college try'. Horrified, his ex-wife sent him back to my mother. That was the first and only time she managed to get him into rehab. The university agreed to cover the cost. But when he came out three months later, hopeful and ready to change, he was manoeuvred into early semi-retirement at the age of forty-five. That same summer, the furniture smugglers kicked us out. In a stroke of grace, my dad found a cottage being sold for cheap by a debt-ridden crystal thrower who was escaping to Wales with her pet pig. Here my parents tried again to build a home.

For the next fifteen years it was mainly my parents, Pandora and me in the fixer-upper that never quite got fixed. Matthew, my mother's eldest, left for university. Emma left to live with her father and his new family in North London. She returned to our house every other weekend to see her little sisters. Kimber was mostly at his mother's house, a mile down the road. We could always count on him to come to our rescue when things went wrong. But his sister Rachel stayed away. She'd been badly traumatised by the night of the 'old college try'. We didn't see her again until she was a teenager.

In the meantime, my mother had found a job teaching writing at a university eighty miles away. This gave her a secure salary but meant that during the academic year she was gone for two nights a week. My dad was the one always at home, braiding our hair, taking us to school, and cooking us dinner. Often, he was calm and quiet and loving. Sometimes he shuffled around the house in a cloud of medicated depression, saying only hello and goodnight. Other times he would not be able to sleep or sit down and made best friends with whoever happened to knock on the door or pass by the house. The lows would usually lead to highs, and he would turn to drink when he couldn't manage any more. When he picked up, it was in secret, behind a closed door, and only when my mother was away. But once he started drinking again, he couldn't stop, and our precarious home life would fall apart.

In a letter to Elizabeth Bishop, Robert Lowell describes coming down from one of his manic episodes: *Gracelessly*, he writes, *like a standing child trying to sit down, like a cat or a coon coming down a tree, I'm getting down my ladder to the moon. I am part of my family again.* My dad's own ladder to the moon led back down to the kitchen table. However glumly he peeled the potatoes or manically he banged the pots, it was his way to redeem himself, to bring order to what he felt inside. Cooking for his family got him through the day.

In spite of his inner chaos, or perhaps because of it, my dad was a man of strict routine. Each morning he woke up at five. He shaved, showered, made a pot of tea. He laid out two small bowls for my sister and me before starting on our packed lunches, methodically assembling the ham, lettuce and mayonnaise between two slices of sweet white bread. Then he'd sit down to read a mystery novel, and, when the paper came, he'd read it through. At seven thirty he'd turn on the news and oven, put in two chocolate muffins, and call upstairs.

'Wake up, girls!' he'd yell, his hoarse American voice piercing our sleep. The older my sister and I got, the longer we would ignore him. But always, when the muffins were almost ready, he'd poke his head around our bedroom door.

'Girls,' he would say, this time gently. 'Time to get up.'

When we finally emerged, puffy-faced, our eyelids still stuck together, the muffins were on plates by the bowls, and a glass milk bottle was on the counter ready for our cereal.

On a Saturday morning, he'd start thinking about his shopping list. The only time in my childhood I ever saw him using a computer was to print out that list. It was a two-page Word document, the first page laid out in three columns, in the order of the supermarket's aisles, and the second with a chart running from Saturday to Friday, on which he planned the weekly meals. My dad would get out his cookbooks and check the cupboard and the fridge, ticking and crossing off ingredients. Saturdays and Sundays were for trying out new recipes. A Claudia Roden tagine. A stew from *The River Cafe Cook Book*. Or old favourites: steak with thin, crispy rosemary potatoes and a red wine sauce; Cumberland sausages with winey mushrooms and cheesy mashed potatoes. Sundays were for slow-cooked stews or some kind of ragù. Mondays were simple meals. Pasta with peas and ham, or roast beef hash. From Tuesday to Thursday, my mother was usually away teaching, and so he cooked something that would last us until she returned.

Minestrone was what he made when my mother wasn't there, and so for my sister and me, his lows were defined by it. We hated, hated, minestrone. Not that it tasted bad. Carrots, celery, macaroni pasta, in a beany broth. Parmesan grated on top. My mother hardly ever got a chance to have it, so it was one of her favourites. What was not to like? But, for Pandora and me, it was everything depressing about our life without her. It was dinners when my dad didn't speak and the two of us bickered at the table. It was how he always cooked enough to last the week in case by Thursday he couldn't get out of bed at all. We had a silent agreement never to invite friends over for dinner on a Wednesday.

If he'd been drinking, minestrone was his sour, stale smell and pale, glassy eyes. It was me and my sister trying to eat it as quickly as we could, the broth and boiled vegetables burning our tongues, him slurring as he ate, the oily soup glistening around the edges of his mouth. Often, we came home from school to find a whole pot of it on the stove, the kitchen clean and two bowls for us ready on the counter, dust motes catching the last of the sun through the skylight, him already drunk in bed.

I remember coming home from school one time to find a pot of minestrone still warm on the burner. I took the lid off to study the tiny cubes of carrots and celery, a week's worth of food – every part of which he had ticked off on his list, gone to the supermarket to buy, and so carefully chopped. I could already taste it in my mouth, like the memory of old vomit. I lifted the pot and slopped the whole thing into the bin.

At times like these, my sister and I would call our mother and she'd rush home, sending Dad to his office at the top of the house to sober up. Over a week of weird, late-night dinners, of hot dogs and potatoes or pasta, she'd listen to our questions and try to explain our father and his troubles. She'd forget the time and get carried away. We'd keep her company, dancing to Steely Dan while she did the dishes. My dad would spend the week recovering in bed, only coming out to go to the toilet or put a banana in the pocket of his worn old green dressing gown.

But the day would always come when the kitchen would again be filled with the scent of slow-cooked onions or something roasting. A mellow jazz CD playing in the background, Bill Evans or Sarah Vaughan. My parents sitting at the kitchen table, talking through the day. By seven thirty, the kitchen would be spotless, with dinner ready on the table. They could make the house so calm and cosy together that there was no place to remember the betrayal and chaos that had come before.

Little Dolphins

My mother sang Greek songs to all her children. She learned them from local children during summers spent with her family on holiday in Naxos. She used to sing them to my sister and me at bedtime. Our favourite was about a man who rode around the world on the back of a dolphin to forget the woman who broke his heart. She would sing the Greek and translate her version of the English as she went.

'*Delfini delfinaki* . . . Astride the little dolphin . . . I travelled around the world to forget you. But I missed you . . .' I loved to hear her sing about the little dolphin but the lovesick man made no sense to me. There was a part of the song where he lamented a stab in the heart. I thought that meant he'd stabbed the dolphin. It always made me so sad. I wished the dolphin could ride away and escape the man.

When my father fell apart – if he picked up drinking and became too crazy for us to share a house with – we lived out a version of this song again and again. 'I've had it. I've just had it,' my mother would say. Last minute and with little or no plans, astride the dolphin of her imagination, she'd take us away and make it look like an adventure.

Usually these trips were to Istanbul, where we would see her parents, now that they had settled there for good. Once we went to Spain in the middle of the school term, to a village where she'd once lived with her ex-husband Paul. We stayed in one of her old friend's houses. A very tall friend who had fitted counters and cupboards and sinks we couldn't reach. We ate tortillas at the beach and stayed up late in the one cafe and were able to forget the stress and sorrows of home for a week in the beautiful, breezy village that had once been her home. Walking up and down the steep climb to the beach, she taught us our times tables. Eight times seven equals fifty-six makes me think of tired legs, windy afternoons, orange trees and purple flowers growing out of stone walls along the path, and so who could ever say I had a difficult childhood?

Really, these trips were also visits back to her own difficult but enchanted childhood. Her Irish-American parents had left New Jersey and moved when she was eight to an American college campus in Istanbul where her father taught physics. Every winter, spring and summer vacation they set off for a new part of the Mediterranean. They had lots of charm and little money and, wherever they went, they took their children with them, usually forgetting they were children, sometimes forgetting their children altogether. Famously, my mother's younger sister was left behind at a petrol station between Cairo and Alexandria when she was six. This was how my mother grew up and it was the kind of life that she believed in. She wanted us to open our eyes to the wider world, so long as we were not in danger, as she had so often been, and so long as we had a home to return to, as she often had not. So we were lucky in one sense, although our adventures were really escapes, flights from our father to whom we would return and find waiting for us, forlorn and broken.

The time I remember the most was when we went all the way to San Francisco for three weeks, a place she had also lived with Emma and Matthew years before. My father had been making terrifying yells in the night, locked up in his study at the top of the house, drinking or coming down from the drink, and she decided we needed a trip away. She called some old friends, bought flights on a credit card and pulled us out of school a week before the Easter holidays. She bought us each a book to record the trip and make it educational. I was seven and hadn't been to America since I was a baby but the most exciting part about this sudden trip was the news that the friend we were staying with had a Dalmatian.

'Is it a girl, Mummy? Does it have black ears or spotty ones or a patch around its eye? Will it be friendly? Mummy?'

Our favourite film was *101 Dalmatians*. Our two cats were named after the main dogs, Pongo and

Perdy. We needed to know everything about this real Dalmatian.

'Am I a mind reader?' she snapped at us when we kept asking her the same questions on the plane. 'Why don't you pass me my phone and I'll call God.' She pulled out the Nokia from her leather handbag wedged between her legs. 'We might crash the plane but at least you will be able to know what colour ears the dog has!' Afraid of her God and the plane crashing we let it go. I opened my new book and wrote on the first page that I was excited to see the Dalmatian. I couldn't think of anything else to say. I closed it again and wrote on the front cover *This is My Holiday* and underlined it twice. Beside me, Pandora did exactly the same.

San Francisco was a haze of pastel houses and rolling roads. From the moment we walked into the first friend's house all thoughts of educational holidays and Dalmatians fell away when it was discovered that my sister and I had nits in our long and tangly hair. And so the next adventure was finding a place we could stay where our nits were at least tolerated. Why didn't she try mayonnaise? Peanut butter? Or cut all our hair off? This was something her friends asked again and again. In America, we discovered, nits were called head lice and our hair might as well have been infested with tiny rats. A week with one friend turned into a stay at a motel, turned into staying with another friend with conditions of mayonnaise and peanut butter and never getting too close to her own children. My sister and I felt dirty and ashamed but the city soon washed our worries away with its foggy beauty and the joy of discovering the end of America and weeks of our mother all to ourselves. Hills as steep as staircases and familiar stop signs and shop signs I had seen before in a dream or a long-lost memory, which was really thousands of afternoons spent glued to American TV shows. There was the prison island and comforting Vietnamese soups and cheerful parks and grey cloudy streets, and when you turned a corner, there was glorious sun. But where was the Dalmatian? 'The fog rolls in here,' my mother kept telling us. 'The fog rolls in and the fog rolls out. That's what the San Franciscans say.' We borrowed a car from a friend who felt guilty about the head-lice problem and drove to a faraway and chilly beach. Pandora and I made up a game to do with running away from the waves. She fell head first into a wave in all her clothes and so the rest of the day was spent driving down huge California roads searching for a place that sold dry pants. It was hours of my sister shivering in the back of the car, bouncing from strip mall to strip mall and the wrong roads to the wrong roads, before we found a Gap outlet off a highway where somehow there were no underpants either but grey shorts that were white and fluffy on the inside and so who needed pants. Our soft shorts, we called them. From that point on we wore them every day.

One afternoon, wandering around the city in our beloved soft shorts, we stumbled on a cafe in which you could paint your own pottery. Pandora painted some white-and-black blobs on a plate and said it was a panda. Our mother painted a coaster with the words *Girls' Trip to San Francisco* written inside a wonky purple heart. I painted a Dalmatian on a dressing jug and wrote *Salad* along the side. I said I'd give it to my dad, who made salad dressing every night.

'Do you miss Daddy?' my mother asked us. Pandora nodded sadly.

'No,' I said. For a moment, her question broke the spell of San Francisco. 'Why would I miss him?'

We were running around beaches in the sun in soft shorts. There was the best aquarium in the world, my mother and her friends said. And in the bay there might even be dolphins. Well there weren't any dolphins but at the end in the gift shop I found a basket full of cuddly toy ones, some grey and some white, like the inside of our soft shorts and the outside. It was very important to me that I had the white fluffy one and that Pandora must have the grey one. Our mother agreed. She said that dolphins were grey so my sister was the real winner – she'd have the most realistic dolphin. My sister did not agree. She said it was very hard to be the youngest and she was never the winner. She cried and cried all the way back to the car. She cried so much she scared all the real little dolphins away from the bay and we never saw them. 'But isn't it nice to go away, honey-bunchie? Haven't you had a wonderful vacation?'

But we had to go home. On the way back to the airport, I remembered again.

'Mummy?' I asked her. 'What happened to the Dalmatian?'

'What?' she said. 'Tell me about my vacation? Oh!' And she started telling the story of our holiday. She seemed so happy to tell her story that we didn't have the heart to correct her. On she went, talking about how much she loved San Francisco, the light, the hills, the cafes where you could paint your own pottery. How she knew it was a little crazy . . . to go so far away when she was always struggling so much with money but it was always worth it. Didn't we think so? To find a way to go somewhere else and have a good time. No matter how bad a day was, there was always a way to appreciate something beautiful by the end of it. To make the best of a bad time. 'That's what my parents taught me. That's what they always did too . . .'

With the soft hum of her voice and the car's wheels on the road, my sister and I rested our nit-infested heads on our mother's lap and fell asleep and began our long journey back across the world.

The light changed, the unhappy airport, the drizzly train with windows to much gloomier clouds. The dark street which led to our house where the lamps were on and jazz was playing from the speakers and my father existed again, cooking an extravagant dinner to welcome us home. The crazy father we left had turned back into the ordinary glum and loving father, but not all the way. His face was worn, his eyes were red-rimmed. He had a few cuts on his chin from shaving and his hands shook as he prepared his usual dressing in the new salad jug I'd painted for him.

'What's that, sweetie?' he asked me, pointing at the white splodge with black dots and pink ears. 'A bunny? A cat?' How could I tell him it was the Dalmatian? I shook my head and could not explain. Where had he been?

'Isn't it nice, girls,' my mother said. 'Coming home, after going away.' She had been so eager to escape and now, as always, she was so happy to see him. The light and sand and fog were pieces of a faraway island that didn't exist any more.

After dinner, our mother put us to bed and sang our song which was really her song.

Across the hallway came the creaks of Dad getting into their bed. Our mother stood and kissed us both goodnight. It was a great tragedy.

'Can you sing it one more time?'

'*Delfini delfinaki* . . . Dolphin, little dolphin. I travelled over the world to forget you but I missed you.'

Quakers at War

When people asked my dad why he'd settled in England, he'd say it was to get away from his family. But he didn't want to be English either — that would betray his Quaker roots which he took very seriously. It had been to escape persecution that the first Longstreths had sailed to Philadelphia with William Penn in 1699. My grandmother's family arrived about a hundred years later. They'd left England so they'd never have to take off their hats in the presence of a king or swear allegiance to him or fight in his wars or be branded or beaten or put in prison for believing that nothing stood between a person and God. My father was ashamed of America's crimes, and to be from such an early settler family, but equally proud that Quakers had always fought against slavery and risked their lives to stand up for equality. Everyone on this earth had a god-like potential, he taught us. An inner light, that connected them to each other and the universe, if we let it.

There was a meeting house in Bath that he took me to occasionally when I was very young. You were supposed to sit silently in a circle and stand to speak when touched by the light of God but he kept standing up to speak only about American politics, until one day a lady shushed him. He came home crushed and never went back again. But the Quakers of his family tree mattered more to him than the shushers of Bath. He had the family genealogies in weighty bound hardbacks for both my grandparents' lines, which he kept propped on a shelf in the corner of the office he never used. Every so often, the light would strike and he'd pull down the book about his mother's family, jab his finger at a random page and say: 'There were two Quaker brothers who lived in England. One stayed and opened a Cadbury factory and the other ran away to Philadelphia so he could marry his cousin.'

He said this like it was funny, but I was spooked by those books. I was worried about what it meant to be descended from cousins marrying cousins. I thought it might be why my skin was always so dry and my hands were so wrinkly. It was not normal for a child to have such wrinkled hands. And it was not normal for my dad to be like he was, like his brother and two sisters were too. So up and so down. So sober, trying to help each other stay sober, and then so not able to stop drinking. Even when phone calls were expensive, he and his two younger siblings spoke almost every day. Building each other up or setting each other off. A bad call from his sister Lucy could leave my dad reeling for weeks. I remember hearing him on the phone to Uncle Kimber once. 'Calm down, Kimber,' he told him. 'You're not broken. You're having a panic attack. You're not broken.'

When he hung up, he turned to my mum and asked, 'What happened to us? We used to be so full of promise and now we are so broken. How did we get to be so broken?'

That question stayed with me and I went to my mum for answers during our late-night hot-dog meals, whenever he was upstairs doing badly. She blamed the pressure all the children were under, especially my father and his brother Kimber, to join the ranks of the great and the good. The generations of privilege and intermarriage, the 1929 Wall Street crash, and the long history of hard drinking, which was so often in secret, because Quakers weren't supposed to drink at all. Most of all she blamed his parents, who she'd never liked and who'd never liked her, because she was Irish, but that was good news for my sister and me because half our genes came from far away from those inbred WASP Quakers. Never mind that she was always saying that on the far western tip of County Kerry where her parents came from, everyone had the same last names and looked identical.

My father's parents, Frank and Patty, were married at the Quaker meeting in Haverford in the middle of the Second World War, just after my grandfather joined the Marines. He even wore his military uniform to the wedding – an odd and controversial thing for a Quaker to do. While he was overseas Patty ran off with a rabbi, divorcing Frank Senior in absentia. For some reason they started seeing each other again after the war, and my grandmother got pregnant and they remarried. Partly to get away from the scandal Frank took a teaching job at a boys' boarding school in Ohio, several hundred miles away from Philadelphia, and they moved to Hudson where my Aunt Helen was born, followed by my father, Kimber and Lucy.

Hudson was a classic small midwestern all-American town. The big events of the year were the Memorial Day parade, the ice-cream social, the tennis club picnic and singing Christmas carols on the town green. The drugstore sold root-beer phosphates and chocolate malts for twenty-five cents and my grandfather had his own key for the pub next door – yet another odd thing for a Quaker.

In many ways my dad had an idyllic American childhood. In the post-war baby boom there were a lot of other boys around his age to play with and they had free use of the school grounds. Life was one long sports event – basketball, swimming, American football, baseball, tennis and soccer. They were always in and out of each other's houses. From a very early age he was mostly just running loose in a pair of shorts and a T-shirt. In the summer he hardly ever wore shoes. His mother would pull him inside once a week and wash his clothes and make sure he had a bath. In the winter his father would pull his children and all their friends inside to play his own infamous version of Monopoly with the rest of the family. The main rule was that you could cheat if you got away with it. It wouldn't be a stretch to say that this was the unspoken rule for the whole neighbourhood, with all its hard drinking and unhappy marriages. His parents never talked to each other, not even to argue. But the silence was easy enough to ignore and the kids thrived. The way people talk about it, they were golden and brilliant and charmed. Everyone thought they were destined for some sort of greatness.

Then one day Dad's ten-year-old brother stumbled on a stash of love letters between their father and a close family friend named Cynthia. He tried to hide them again but his mother found them anyway, so the story goes. When she confronted his father, she lied and said Kimber had brought the letters straight to her. She then sent Kimber to the school incinerator with the trash. His father, drunk and furious, chased after him. Holding him up over the flames, he'd accused him of destroying their family.

The first my dad heard of this was when his mother came into his bedroom that night, after yet another silent supper. It happened to be the same day he found out he'd won a scholarship to Harvard. She told him of the affair and said she was leaving for Philadelphia in the morning, and then she went to bed. It was his job to tell his two younger siblings that they were going with her. Dad's first thought was that he was very stupid, not to have seen this coming. All four of Cynthia's children were best friends with my dad and his younger siblings, and her eldest daughter was actually Dad's girlfriend at the time. It was quite common for him to be hanging out in the sitting room with his girlfriend and soon-to-be stepsister and various other friends with his father popping in and out. He never thought to question it. I suppose now he started to question everything.

After a strange and dismal summer spent with his father in a half-empty house, he left for university. By Christmas his parents were divorced and his father was remarried and Cynthia had moved into the house with her four children. Back in Haverford, his mother was drinking heavily and in such bad shape that my dad almost dropped out of college to look after Lucy and Kimber but, at the last minute, Helen Cadbury, the grandmother I'm named after, stepped in and hooked her up with another man, who was what's more another Quaker Latin teacher. This one was wealthy, widowed and childless. He hated his new stepchildren and they hated him too. Lucy went so far as to go to court at fifteen years old and divorce her mother so that she and her younger brother Kimber could move back to Hudson. My grandmother never stopped hating my grandfather, who was not to be mentioned in her presence. Never mind that my father had been named after him and looked just like him. My grandfather liked to joke to his children: 'The worst mistake I ever made in my life was marrying your mother – twice!' He did truly love Cynthia, who worked hard to embrace all eight children as her own for the rest of her too-short life. But after she died there was a series of unsuitable girlfriends, uniformly derided by all the siblings and step-siblings.

There was no end to the warfare, which spilled over into the next generation, as my father and his siblings had their own dramas, divorces and alcohol-fuelled bipolar breakdowns, communicated by telephone. My brother Kimber (named after Uncle Kimber who was named after their grandfather Thomas Kimber) believed there was a family curse. There was a picture from one of those spooky family-tree books that proved it to me – a formal portrait of my great-grandmother, Ella Hoover. She'd been a leader in the temperance movement, smashing up saloon windows with a club. In this picture she had a dead fox around her shoulders with sewed-up eyes. Her own eyes were black and round with eerie glints. I thought she had taken the fox's eyes and was now wearing them.

I was eight when we made our first trip to visit Dad's America. It was 1999, soon to be the millennium, and my dad was manic. He was turning fifty and had decided he needed to see his family. He said it was an emergency, the fucking world might end. There was probably never going to be a good time to do a big family visit but I know now that this was a particularly bad time. His father, seven years since Cynthia had tragically died, had just taken up with a hateful younger woman who was selling the family heirlooms on newly established eBay. He wasn't talking to his sister Helen for refusing to corroborate memories she had recovered under hypnosis about a satanic neighbour. His newly divorced and struggling-to-be-sober sister Lucy had just married a born-again alcoholic, and his unmarried brother Kimber, the family's undisputed star – formerly Teddy Kennedy's top arms-control negotiator, currently the highest-ranking Quaker in the Pentagon – had become embroiled in the Monica Lewinsky scandal, after it came out in her biography that he'd got her pregnant, little knowing that she was having an affair with the president at the same time. The media had been camping out outside his house in Arlington on and off all year. He had always been a heavy-drinking workaholic. Disgraced by association, his career was unravelling and he'd been filling the gap with vodka.

Unsurprisingly, my mother thought the trip would be a nightmare. My dad was already unstable, but he was so worried about his siblings and so desperate to help them that there was no reasoning with him. And Kimber, his only son, was living there now and would be turning twenty. And *he* was turning fifty. And the fucking world might end. And the airfare was cheap because of the millennium-bug panic.

And then there we were, at the top of a world that had not ended yet, in a penthouse in Manhattan, where my dad's youngest stepsister Annie lived rent-free with her two kids and now my brother Kimber, because the place belonged to a family friend. Annie had long golden hair, arms full of bangles, and leopard-print leggings. The fridge was stocked full of SunnyD and Korean takeout. The kitchen faced downtown, with a window that framed the Twin Towers. My dad's stepsister Elizabeth, who had once been his girlfriend, was visiting from California with her husband and two kids. Uncle Kimber had flown up from Washington DC. He was handsome and bright-eyed, just like he had been described to me, in high spirits with a bag full of gifts and stories about jetting around on Air Force One on missions he kept quiet with a shy throwaway wave. He was also just an ordinary uncle in a collared bomber jacket, white trainers, and hair combed to the side. He took me in an arm and ruffled my hair. He didn't look like a broken person at all. Nobody did. They were shining bright, teasing each other, talking about the old times, arms clapped around backs, with the Twin Towers lit up in the window behind them. My mum couldn't get a word in. There were long carpeted corridors and big leather sofas and cousins falling on top of cousins. We ran up and down the six flights of stairs, playing chase until Pandora was sick on the landing.

In Florence, Massachusetts, with Aunt Lucy for the millennium, there was another living room filled with cousins. Lucy was so excited to see us that she could not sit down to eat the meal she'd spent days preparing. My dad was so excited he couldn't sit down either. There was the *South Park* millennium special playing on the TV set that caused a big fight between Lucy and my father and Lucy's newborn addict husband when Jesus inserted a tampon. At midnight, my mother had the idea to run around the house banging pots and pans, because that was how she and her friends had always celebrated the New Year in Istanbul. We ran around the quiet suburban neighbourhood waiting for the world to end. It didn't but by the next day it was clear that both Lucy and my dad had begun drinking in secret. They locked themselves away all day and we were stranded. Our cousins' father came to take them away, and a deathly quiet fell over the house. Who knows how we spent the next few days but, by my dad's birthday on the 6th of January, he and his sister had pulled themselves together and we all went to a seafood restaurant. They gave my dad a bib that had an illustration of a lobster eating another lobster and he ordered two. 'I'm fifty and the fucking world didn't end,' he told us. 'So I'm having two lobsters.'

In Hudson, Ohio, there was thick snow, picket fences and white wooden houses with green shutters. A big, bearded man who knew my dad's stepsister Tori waved and welcomed us to America from the seat of his truck. There were flying flags and placards. There was the prep school across the street from the house where my dad grew up. There were even more cousins and these cousins had a GameCube. The drugstore still sold rootbeer phosphates. The local bar on Main Street had a plaque for my grandad. In Aunty Tori's sprawling living room, just around the corner from the school and the old house, my grandad was a looming but strangely diminished presence, presiding over the generations from a giant sofa with Susan, the hated girlfriend. The two Franks looked just like each other, except that one was older and more frightening. They posed for a photo and fought to give each other bunny ears behind each other's heads. It seemed they were fighting over who got to be Frank and my dad kept losing, like he'd been born to lose, like that had always been the point.

All across the country, as I saw it, my beloved newfound cousins were playing GameCube and drinking SunnyD and jumping around in living rooms filled with giant sofas. But we had to leave them all behind and move on to my grandmother's retirement community in Haverford, on the outskirts of Philadelphia. The building was a converted mansion with red carpets, dark-panelled walls and a grand staircase spiralling above the reception desk. Granny was waiting for us in the silent lobby with her third husband, Bill Thomas, who had huge white eyebrows and very kind eyes and held Granny's cold purple hands the whole time that we sat with them. My father was so blown out from the trip by this point that he could barely talk. After dinner, he went straight to the guest suite behind the reception and didn't get up for the next few days, once again leaving us stranded with nothing to do but wander the airless corridors and find TVs and count wheelchairs and turn up at five p.m. sharp at the grill that had a sign by the door listing all the residents who'd died that week. The place was the haunted inverse of all the bright and noisy living rooms full of arguments and life and family I'd seen in America so far. As soon as we were seated, Granny would ask my mother where her son was, and she would tell the truth: her son was in bed. Granny would say, 'Well. I don't know why you keep coming down here without him.'

On the last day my Uncle Kimber drove up from Washington. The fun uncle I'd met in New York had burned out. He had the same blurred look in his eye which I knew in my dad and had also seen now in Lucy. But when my dad finally got out of bed to greet him, his face lit up and they threw their arms around each other. They both seemed beyond speech. At lunch Granny joined them in their silence, while her kind new husband and my mother did their best to keep things cheerful. At the end of the meal, Uncle Kimber jumped up and said, 'Let's go visit Granny's grave.'

Off we went through the dusk to the graveyard beside Haverford Meeting where my grandparents had married, twice, all those years ago and where most of their relatives had also married and been buried. Etched into the plain flat headstones were all our names. Helens and Kimbers and Franklins and Lucys and Cadburys and Longstreths. We stood before Helen Cadbury's grave and

Uncle Kimber cried. He told us that this was where he wanted to be buried, in the empty plot beside his grandmother. 'She was always so good to me.' My mum asked me how it felt, to be standing beside my namesake. 'What do you think she'd say if she could meet you?' I remember looking at my first two names on the stone. Helen Cadbury. Helen Cadbury. It was too much for my little head to deal with. The names and graves and Granny's unhappy face whenever my dad didn't turn up for dinner. Frank and Kimber and Lucy and my missing Aunt Helen. Inner light and unspoken sorrow and graves.

It was almost five o'clock by now. Time to meet Granny at the grill for our final meal before we ended this whirlwind and went home. We got into our car and Uncle Kimber got into his car. My dad drove us back to the retirement home and my uncle drove off in the other direction and never returned. That was the last we saw of him. My dad would return to America for a few more emergencies – when his father died of heart failure and then when Uncle Kimber died of drink a year later. But we would never visit as a family again.

Plaits

There were so many mornings like this one . . . a lady on the radio reporting faraway disasters, a steaming mug of tea on the kitchen table, ham and lettuce sandwiches in sandwich bags on the counter and a lit cigarette resting on my father's ashtray, while he put my hair into plaits.

'Rumpelstiltskin! Rumpelstiltskin! How to brush such hair of straw?'

He'd pull at my tangles and I'd complain but he took his time with the plaits, studying the first one before moving on to the other, splitting the next section in three, lacing the strands together. I watched the ash grow, eating up the paper until it was a perfect cone. There were so many mornings like this but it was always shocking to see the cone collapse upon itself so suddenly. He'd tie the end of the plait with a little hairband, pat me on the back and say, 'All right, go get your school things ready, we need to leave soon.' Then he'd pick up what little was left of his cigarette and take a happy drag.

Midsummer Dream

Sometimes my mother locked my father out. Once she changed the locks. Occasionally my mother, my sister and I stayed at the Wheatcrofts' house – close family friends on the other side of Bath where we were always welcome and didn't have to answer any questions. There was a period where my sister and I lived with a woman in the village on the days that my mother was at the university, in case my dad picked up drinking. Sometimes nothing happened and we lived together in ordinary harmony but the next sometime was always around the corner and I paid attention to the signs.

In the summer of my last year in primary school something new happened. My mother picked Pandora and me up from school with the bad news that she had returned from the university that afternoon to discover that my father had bolted the door from the inside and locked us out of the house. She told us this very matter-of-factly but she was upset. 'What the hell are we supposed to do?' We walked towards the house and tried again. She knocked and knocked and knocked. I rested my mini scooter on the door. My mum called through the letter box. I looked through the letter box. I could see the black-and-white tiled hallway, could see the poor cat, could see the back door closed and the dark staircase. Our pants and socks and school clothes . . . so near but so far. We gave up and left for the Wheatcrofts'.

Scooting around their long kitchen table, playing Traffic Lights with Abs and Gabes while their mother Sal cooked, and my mother talked at her. Geoffrey was in the next room, shouting at the races on the TV. Round and round the kitchen roundabout we went, stopping at certain chairs, waiting patiently until the invisible lights went red, orange, green and we carried on scooting. Pandora, Abs and I dressed as teenagers, with socks in our bras. And Abs's brother wearing a red curly perm wig and torn-up Che Guevara T-shirt.

'That's quite a look, Gabes,' my mother said.

'What look?' asked Gabes, scooting behind her chair.

Geoffrey shuffled in. 'Some more wine, Maureen?' He opened the fridge door right in the middle of the road.

'Move, old man!' Abs said.

'Oh what a horrible child you are!' Geoffrey cried out. Sal opened the oven and shook the potatoes.

'I can't believe Frank has gone this far,' my mother said to Sally. I was embarrassed that she was even talking about it. Sally said we could stay as long as we needed.

The next day, I received the bad news that instead

of Helena or Hermia or Titania I had got the part of Narrator 3 in our Year 6 *A Midsummer Night's Dream*. When my mother picked us up from school I was beside myself.

'It isn't good for you,' she said, taking me in her arms. 'Young girls growing up in this constant cycle of hope and disappointment.'

The temporary solution to our forever problem came the next afternoon in the playground. Alison, the mother of a boy in my class – Theo, who'd got the part of Oberon, the Fairy King – offered her barn to us for the month of July.

So the day after that, instead of turning left towards our house or the Wheatcrofts' house, we turned right. Further and further into the valley. The small cottages became bigger ones. The hedge-lined road became a narrow country lane with rolling green hills curving out on either side. Green and glittering leaves rushed past the windows. My mother drove down a narrow lane canopied by dark trees and parked beside a little wooden footbridge that went over a brook, a brook that trickled past a barn-like building and down to a beautiful stone house. The front door was already open and Alison came out from inside, smiling, to welcome us.

The barn was not really a barn. It had heated floors, whitewashed walls, a wetroom shower. Fresh paint, fresh air, a breath of fresh air in a building. At the back, a wide picture window looked out on to the valley, flooding the space with golden, leafy light. There was a sink, a mini fridge, a long table and a fruit bowl with orange and apple and mango sunsets. Upstairs was one beamed room with two made-up twin beds and a sofa. Because there was no cooker, on that first night my mother prepared cold supermarket chicken and a pepper salad. She smiled and the peppers crunched in her mouth.

'You know, Alison's brother is an alcoholic. I didn't need to explain too much. She understands.'

Outside, the youngest of Alison's children appeared at the window.

'Can Helen and Pandora come out to play?'

Behind the bush where Maud stood, her older brother Theo was bouncing and doing flips on the trampoline, shouting out his lines: 'Ill met by moonlight, proud Titania!'

And I thought if only, if only, I had been Titania and not Narrator Number 3.

From then on, in the morning, after school and after dinner, Maud would pop her little head up at the window above the door and my sister and I would go out. We'd hunt crayfish in the brook, make dance routines on the trampoline, play elaborate games of hide and seek around the huge garden. Theo would be somewhere in the distance, not quite able to engage, not quite able to hide away inside, wandering between the front door and the side door and the back door of his house, maybe going up to the tree house, maybe practising flips on the trampoline, always with bare feet and his head bent down, drumming on his leg, often with some item of food in his hand. 'Whenever I see you, you're always eating!' I would say. 'Shut up, you idiot' was his usual response.

For dinner my mother prepared her cold chicken and mixed pepper salad dressed in oil and vinegar. Our feet warmed on the heated flooring. For breakfast, sliced mango. 'I could eat this every day!' she'd say. And we did. The sun went away at night and came back in the morning. Emma came up for the weekend and we had trifles for breakfast too. 'Such a nice summer we're having!' people said in passing on the walk to school. Instead of lessons we practised the play under the gazebo, or drew, or painted, or wrote stories. Theo as Oberon in his Gap hoodie, bellowing: 'Ill met by moonlight, proud Titania!' Charlie as the fairy Puck, crouched in the grass, hopping frog-like: 'Lord, what fools these mortals be!' Helena, down on her knees: 'Spurn me, strike me, neglect me, lose me!' Hermia, calling over her shoulder: 'The more I hate, the more he follows me.' Lysander, letting loose his heartfelt cry: 'The course of true love never did run smooth!' Me, and Narrators 1, 2 and 4, spinning on and off to tell the story the way Shakespeare never intended: 'Demetrius loves Hermia but Hermia loves Lysander and Hermia's friend Helena loves Demetrius. Be quiet, here they come . . .' And I almost forgot about my dad, just down the road in his mystery midlife midsummer nightmare.

When our mother arrived at the end of the day, with

quick steps to the school gate, we'd run to her. She'd tell us that our dad was clearing himself up now, that he was so ashamed with himself and wanted us to come back home or come over for dinner. My sister would say nothing and seem not to be listening and I'd tell Mum, no, we didn't want to see him or hear any more about it, and we'd turn right not left at the top of School Lane. 'Sunshine really makes a difference, doesn't it?' people said in passing on our walk through the valley. The grass was turning yellow. Back at the barn we played until dinner and after dinner we played until it was dark. On the weekends, Sal drove Abs over and we made up dances on the trampoline. We played cards on the trampoline. We lay out on the trampoline and read our new hardback copies of *Harry Potter and the Order of the Phoenix*. We looked for Theo. He revealed that Sirius Black dies at the end of the book and Maud cried. He jumped on the trampoline and destroyed our card game. He told us about Pig Head Man who haunted the corridors of St Catherine's Court and the soldier ghost who roamed the corridors of another house down the road – the same house that was completely covered with moss in the middle of the night, even the fish bowl! Maud said he was a liar and just stealing stories from a ghost-story book she'd seen him reading and Theo threw a burger bun at her head and stormed off to his mother's kitchen.

    Hot evenings, hot bugs, flying insects, the longest days just rambling along as the brook rambled from the village to the barn to the house and on into the valley. At night, I imagined Theo might be waiting outside the barn. I imagined he might throw something at the window by my bed. 'Ill met by moonlight, proud Titania!' I'd sneak out and we'd meet in the tree house to . . . kiss? Hug? Fall asleep holding hands? I'm not sure what I hoped for at age eleven. But it all seemed like something hopeful was building and gathering, one detail on top of another, one leaf on top of another, a countryside of trees. Insects skimming the pond by the house, making ripples on the water; the water reflected the leaves and the veiny undersides of the leaves reflected the rippling water. Sometimes I felt that all the rippling was happening inside me, under my skin too. That if I stared at a leaf too long I might fall into it. If I looked too hard at anything I would be inside it. If I stared at the blond-brown hairs on Theo's head long enough they might tell me about what the hell was going on in there and if he wanted to meet up in the middle of the night too.

So when the day finally came – the last night at the barn and the first and only night of the play – I don't know, how else to say it? I was disappointed. Chairs were arranged in a semicircle on the tarmac. A painting of trees on a cloth was tied up across a wooden climbing frame. We four narrators sat frozen in our places in the front row, dressed as sprites with green paint on our faces and gold in our hair. We were supposed to be statues. I watched my dad arrive through the school gates. It had only been a month but he was so skinny and so pale, a moon under his skin. 'Hi, sweetie! Hello!' he said and his gaunt moon-face smiled at me brightly. I remained a statue. My mother arrived behind him. They found their seats. Tears rose and lingered mysteriously around the bottom of my eyeballs. I blinked them away and the play began.

Narrator 1 twirled out on to the tarmac stage. 'Ladies and gentlemen, girls and boys. Please take your seats. And the play will begin. An old story that never gets old, filled with magic and mischief, love and heartbreak, sadness and joy.' The audience applauded. The narrator twirled off. On came the king's messenger to tell the king about a play. On came Narrator 2. On came the fairies, the lovers and the play within the play. I twirled on to the stage for my big moment: 'Puck pours the love juice in the wrong lover's eye. Now thanks to his meddling the lovers are in disarray. Now it is Hermia who loves Demetrius and it is both Demetrius and Lysander who love . . . who love . . .' I froze onstage and forgot my line. In the audience my dad stood up, mouthing something and pointing at me. 'Your name!' he shouted. 'Who loves . . . Helena!' I said finally and twirled off. He sat down, pleased, and the show carried on. Helena chased Demetrius. Hermia slapped Helena. Hermia latched herself to Lysander's knees. Lysander kicked Hermia away. Puck turned Bottom into a donkey. Titania chased Bottom through the woods. Demetrius and Lysander fought. Demetrius accidentally whacked Hermia in her recently developed boobs. The fairies made a fog and the lovers wandered around the stage blindly, calling out the wrong lovers' names. 'LORD, WHAT FOOLS THESE MORTALS BE!' cried Puck, before pouring the love juice in the rightful lovers' eyes, telling the audience that he would make amends and take back all his meddling. How soon the lovers would wake up, be in love with their rightful partners, and think it had all been just a bad dream.

The play was over. The play was a hit but it was over. My dad was recovered. We would stay a few more nights at the barn and then we would go home.

At the end of the evening, we left our dad at the top of School Lane. He turned left to go home and we turned right. I didn't want to go back to our life, but watching him head off in the other direction, so skinny now and all alone . . . what else could we do? We held our mum's hand and headed through the valley to enjoy our last few nights.

New Blood Wedding

'Love is what you've been through with someone.' My mother often said this, especially during the rocky times — a line she said came from her first husband's father.

It made sense as a justification for our family story, with all the broken marriages, bad divorces, traumatised children and parents falling to pieces — a lot of people going through something which conveniently was also Love. But as a young teenager who had never been in love, I couldn't get my head around it. 'What you've been through' seemed to me a definition that looked backwards, making sense of what had already happened, rather than something that could be happening now, any day now, just around the corner, as soon as possible, please. I just wanted to fall in love myself. I wanted: 'I am Heathcliff!' I wanted to hold Satine's dead body at the end of *Moulin Rouge*, to cry out into oblivion and know what that loss felt like. I wanted to go through something with someone but for that something to be a shared dream, rather than some kind of excuse.

And yet, these first years of secondary school were the most peaceful at home. My dad was mostly sober. For the first time, my life was not dictated by the worries and consequences of his drinking but by normal teenager worries and disappointments. Bad hair and bad skin and best friends and fallouts and cat hair on my school uniform and would I ever get a boyfriend? Walking up the hill from school one afternoon, listening to my best friend Sally complain about how she was falling behind at school because of all the arguments she was having with her boyfriend, I said: 'But love is doing your homework together!' It just slipped out and Sally teased me but I secretly stood by what it meant. The side-by-side everyday harmony of love – that simple and yet elusive bliss, the comfort of company alongside the peace of solitude, making something together . . . that was what I longed for the most.

I knew my parents were in love, even with all my dad's troubles, and I suppose I grew up to understand that great love was an answer to something. I once asked them how many times they'd been in love. My mother was cagey, she didn't know, she said it was usually people falling in love with her. My father said with confidence that he'd fallen in love hundreds of times, sometimes once a week. Oh dear. I knew that was going to be me. It was always a little scary to have so much in common with my dad.

When I was sixteen, the peaceful years ended. First my dad's father died. Less than a year later came the news that his brother was dying from organ failure. There were two disastrous trips to America, after which he was no longer talking to his remaining siblings, and that spring he had a series of serious relapses, which rocked our home life and landed him in hospital with a severe stomach ulcer. He almost died too and was there three days for blood transfusions. When he returned home, pumped full of someone else's blood, for a while he became a different person. New Blood Frank, we called him.

New Blood Frank was in love with life and not in the aggressive finger-pointing way that usually came after a bad slump. He had come back from death springing, filled with more love and blood than he had ever had in him. Kissing my mother, kissing his children on each cheek. Kissing the cheeks of confused neighbours in passing like a jolly drunk peasant, except he wasn't drinking. He'd forgotten all about that problem because he was a new person.

And it was New Blood Frank who one afternoon at the start of June took his beating heart for a trip to town and found himself booking a slot for a marriage for the 4th of July, without telling anyone, not even my mother. His first call was to firstborn Kimber, who'd taken the news straight to my mother's first daughter, Emma, as they were close and living near each other in North London at the time. Emma had got straight on the phone to rage at our mother, who was on a train home after a long day of teaching and didn't know a thing about it. 'But, Frank,' she said to her newly deflated future husband when she came in the door, exasperated and not excited as he had hoped. 'It's in two weeks and you didn't even propose!'

But by the next day, she was on board. They were getting married! It made sense for them to be married. What if he really died? Or she died? What would happen to the house? They were not protected in the eyes of the law and so they might as well get married and have a big party. They wanted all their children there. Wasn't it funny that there was a slot open for the 4th of July when they were Americans? They joked that their children were too English and didn't get it. We children were no longer children and were upset about the whole thing, especially Emma who said she was busy that day and was not going to come. There had been the relapses all spring, every time my mother was teaching, with Pandora and I having to stay at friends' houses during my A level exams. Then he'd almost died. Then he'd come back alive as an insufferable New Blood romancer and now they were getting married? All in a couple of weeks? I didn't care about the date, 4th of July or not. I just hated that it was happening and couldn't pretend to be happy about it or catch sight of them walking around the garden hand in hand and think it was cute like Pandora did.

It was a June afternoon after school, that same June of New Blood Frank, when I first saw the person I'd been saving up all my love for. I was waiting at the bus stop across from the Guildhall, and he was across the road, walking in the opposite direction, carrying a large maroon sketchbook . . . the most beautiful boy I'd ever seen. He didn't see me, he wasn't looking for me, he didn't seem to be noticing the street at all. He seemed to be already wherever he was going, which was somewhere, and that somewhere I decided was where I was destined to be too. Walking hand in hand through town . . . drawing in his sketchbook while I did my English literature homework beside him, oh how sweet, he was sketching me while I read. He disappeared behind the abbey and I missed him. The bus arrived and I sat at the top, totally shook. So this was it. I had fallen in love. Just around the corner and good thing I had been looking. What a relief!

Passages in books, the most romantic love scenes, the best songs for heartbreak. Best songs for unrequited love, best songs for first love. While my parents were planning the last-minute wedding that no one wanted to go to, I was researching. You had me at hello. Love is like oxygen. Love lifts you up where you belong! The scene in *The Girl Next Door* where the boy and the girl next door kiss and the camera spins around them to the wailing of David Gray. *A Room with a View:* 'Something tremendous has happened,' says George to Lucy – to the one he suddenly loves. She resists and they find themselves in a field of violets. The Italian chauffeur shouts: 'Courage! . . . Courage and love!'

And didn't it mean something that I was suddenly

seeing this boy everywhere? Once in town with Abs. Another time by the boys' school when Sally and I were walking her dog. And finally a third time at the bar of the Nest. He told me that his name was Henry.

'Have you ever had an alcoholic Dr Pepper?' he asked me.

The barman poured Coke, amaretto, rum, the sun, the moon and stars into a tall glass over ice.

'Wow. It tastes just like Dr Pepper!' I said and he smiled. His eyes were incredibly blue. I grazed his hand and he took mine back.

'You have really nice eyes,' I said.

'So do you!'

Was it a dream? He added me on Facebook. Was it a dream that life was suddenly full of such hope and such pain? The sun and shade from trees along the pavement, the shadow of every bus stop, the sun on my face as I stepped over the other side. The birds were singing and there was a creepy crow scuttling along my windowsill every morning. Downstairs my father was singing and it was a terrible sound, but I didn't mind because someone out there existed and he was the one I had been waiting for.

It was a crazy New Blood start to the summer. One morning there was the newsagent in the garden and my dad was showing him all the new plants. One afternoon my sister and my dad were baking baked Alaska. Neil Young was playing from the CD player in the garden most days and nights. Old man, old man, take a look at your life, take a look at my life. I avoided my dad and his crazy good mood and instead was thinking of Henry non-stop constantly. I woke up with his name on my pillow and his face on my Golden Grahams in the morning and I loved him. I would love him for ever. I was struck and there was nothing I could do about it, or wanted to do about it. Another afternoon my dad came home from town looking sheepish with something behind his back, which he hid behind the chair in my mother's office. Pandora and I snooped inside, imagining this was his inevitable fallback into sneaking bottles, and instead discovered that it was an Ann Summers bag containing a disturbing lacy outfit. The woman on the front had a red wig and long legs in fishnet. 'Gross!' We pushed the bag further behind the chair. One Thursday night I saw Henry again at the same bar and we kissed. He asked if I wanted to meet up with him in town sometime. I did! He smiled. We kissed again. He had to go . . . his friends were waiting. My other love-obsessed friend Yazzie and I walked home hand in hand, skipping, listening to love songs with one headphone each. In the morning we were rushing a piece of toast before catching the bus to school and my dad came in through the back door, topless and sweaty from working in the garden, to microwave his cup of tea.

'Yazzie, it's Groundhog Day,' he said. 'Yazzie, it's Groundhog Day . . . Yazzie, it's Groundhog Day . . . Yazzie, it's Groundhog Day.'

'Dad, stop! What are you talking about!'

Yazzie was laughing so he carried on a few more times: 'Yazzie, it's Groundhog Day . . . Yazzie, it's Groundhog Day . . .' until finally the tea was warm again and he went back into the garden, laughing to himself.

'Your dad is in a good mood.'

'I told you,' I said. 'It's the New Blood!'

We left and Yazzie noticed me smiling to myself at the bus stop and laughed. 'I think someone else has a case of the New Blood too.'

Courage and love! Courage and love! Would there be a message this morning? Would there be a message online when I came home from school? Might there be a message after I went downstairs and got a biscuit? Maybe if I got another biscuit and prayed.

'What are you doing?' my dad asked me, reading the paper, smiling in his chair beside his special biscuits cabinet.

'Nothing! Stop asking me.'

Was there any god or demon listening? By the time I was back upstairs would there be a message saying: *Hey, would you like to meet up in town sometime?*

'Why don't you just ask him yourself,' Yazzie said when I called her in tears.

'No . . . What would I say?'

'Just ask him if he will be out on Friday?'

'I think that sounds too keen.'

'Just do it!'

★

Friday the 4th of July was a glorious summer's day. New Blood Frank woke up with the magpies and the crows and the blackbirds to decorate the garden with American flags. He hung up all his anti-American T-shirts from the trees too. My brothers Kimber and Matthew were there in suits, setting up the tables. Rachel was going to meet us at the town hall. Emma was not going to come. My mother's parents arrived from Istanbul. None of my father's family were able to make it at the last minute but his best friend came all the way from Boston for just two days. Pandora wore a black dress, I wore white and my mother wore red . . . not to make a point, but I guess we just hadn't been to many weddings.

Despite everything, we were all in a good mood. My parents were handsome and happy, the sun was shining. Henry had not responded to me, but I wasn't thinking about it for a morning, just for the morning. We piled into a taxi and showed up at the Guildhall. My mother walked down the aisle with her father, buffeted by the discordant horns of the World Saxophone Quartet. Then a hush fell over the room as an American friend read from Thoreau's *Walden* : 'When first I took up my abode in the woods . . . which, by accident, was on Independence Day, or the Fourth of July.'

Back at the house, my friends and I were in charge of pouring the wine, stumbling around the garden in our high heels. One for you, one for me. And for my siblings and my cousins it was one bottle for you, one bottle for you . . . Green grass, blue sky. Red, white, blue and anti-American T-shirts fluttering in the breeze. A very yellow vat of coronation chicken and its picked remains on paper plates, littered across the garden. My oldest friend Abs, so drunk and wandering around in a child's straw hat. Her boyfriend was now Theo, and he was not being nice to her. A woman said: 'I think you should take that off. That hat is not yours.' There was a wedding gift that was a cactus in the shape of a balls and a penis and Sally made us all take photos posing beside it. I heard my mother tell a friend: 'My idea of Bohemia is finding strange ways to love and appreciate life. That's what you use your creativity towards . . .' Women who had been hippies once gathered my friends and me in a circle, pointing to our shoes and asking us why? Why after all their hard work did girls still want to wear high heels? A friend of my father's that I'd never liked told me that Frank was a great guy and I should be nicer to him. After many hours, my friends and I stumbled into town for Grace's seventeenth birthday party. Pretty soon, those in couples peeled off one by one to have drunken arguments. Abs and Theo disappeared down an alley. Sally threw up on her boyfriend's new trainers and he shoved her in a taxi. I was busy looking for the love of my life. I dragged Yazzie to the pub where I first met him, then to another pub, down side streets, up to the Royal Crescent, but he was nowhere to be found.

'Just give up,' Yazzie said. I got in a taxi and sobbed myself all the way home.

★

I woke up on the 5th of July to Abs getting into my bed. Her usually beautiful face was red and swollen from crying too. She said she'd left Theo's house that morning because they'd continued to fight all through the night. She was still drunk and struggling to piece it all together.

'Apparently I was crying for all the children in the world. Apparently I kept trying to get him to take me to a church. He said I ruined his night. He's so angry at me . . .'

She closed her eyes and drifted back off to sleep. Now it was my turn to feel ashamed. It seemed a bad sign I'd not found Henry and an even worse sign I'd dragged Yazzie across the city centre looking for him. I opened up my computer and finally there it was, a message from Henry, saying sorry for the late reply. He was going to be away for the rest of the summer but did I want to meet up when he came back?

Shame and hope and shame. And my father did not get out of bed that morning or the next or the next. He wasn't drinking but the crash was immense, tremendous. He was too depressed to do anything more than sleep and read mystery novels in bed. Seemed he would never get out of bed again. All the while, my mother was making sure he was eating, buying him new mystery books, organising appointments with the doctor. It was July and New Blood Frank had already gone, just as suddenly as he had arrived, just like I knew he would, but it didn't feel good to be right. I'd prepared myself but the sight was still heartbreaking. I felt very guilty and stupid that I had not appreciated his good mood when it was here.

My mother, on the other hand, took it in her stride. She was as easily swept up as she was let down. On the outside she remained the same – pleasant, preoccupied, and closed off, but happy to talk about it all with the distance of wisdom as if it was just someone else's story she was telling. She told me that loving an addict, you learn to appreciate the good times, knowing that they never last. 'Such hope and hopelessness. Well, that's what love is.'

Hopeless, hopeless, hope. And now I would have to wait a whole summer for Henry to come back. And then I would have to wait for him to ask me out and then I would have to wait for him to reply or want to meet up again or call me back or let me down or love me. I would grow pale and ill and eventually die after a life of helpless hopeful waiting but I didn't see any other option because I was in love.

Fleas

The summer before I left for university, our house caught fleas. I slept on a mattress on the floor then so it was very easy for them to just hop right on board. At night in a state of itchy delirium I'd pull my covers off, turn the lamp on and watch the tiny beasts jumping jumping.

We had one cat left by then. Pongo, a scrawny, scrappy thing with a black patch on his eye and an unhappy knotted face. His sister Perdy died earlier that year. When we got them as kittens, Pongo, the runt, had been my cat. He was edgy and skittish, just like me apparently, while Pandora's cat was calm and cuddly, just like her. I wanted Pongo to be my best friend but he ran out of the cat flap if I came near him too quickly and would never be held, even as we all got older. Sometimes he cuddled up to Perdy but that was it. Perdy, soft fur, purring, always jumping on laps. She was easy to love.

Do cats mourn? It seemed like Pongo did. He'd be out even more than usual. We wouldn't see him for days at a time. Who knows where he went, only that he kept bringing fleas to all the soft furnishings and then leaving again.

I was seeing a boy called Kips that summer. He had just graduated with a biology degree but he wanted to be a musician so he'd moved back to the village outside of Bath where we both lived to work at his parents' restaurant for the year. After his shifts in town he'd cycle past my house to deliver leftover desserts. A crème brûlée or a lemon tart. Sometimes he'd bring two and we'd eat them together on my mattress. Other times he'd just hand me a pudding in a little ramekin and bike away to go make up songs. I always felt relaxed with Kips. When he came over I wasn't embarrassed about the fleas or how he would emerge from my mattress with bites across his legs. I think to make me feel better he said he didn't mind. He was a biology graduate after all. He said he was happy to give them his blood so they could keep living. This made Sally and Yazzie laugh. Of course he said that, they said. As if getting bitten by a flea was an act of charity! On one of the few nights he stayed over I turned on the lamp and showed him the fleas jumping jumping. 'Look!' I said. I really wanted him to look at them.

I would probably have lived peacefully with the fleas if it wasn't for how itchy the bites were. I washed my sheets in bleach. I sprayed Pongo's fur. I put a flea collar on him while he scratched up my arms. I cleaned the room and set off toxic flea bombs. None of it worked. In the end what it took to escape the fleas was to leave for university.

Those first months at Manchester . . . I spent them

in bed mostly, with the curtains closed. I lived in a tiny room, with breeze-block walls painted a sickly lime green that I covered with pictures of my friends from home. There was a single bed, a desk, a wardrobe and a window with a view to a tower block where other students lived. The blackout curtains were decorated with a green-and-yellow checked pattern that was like something a computer threw up. The rain was constant. The sun barely rose. I kept the door and window and curtains closed. Not even bugs got in. When I did make it outside, something would go wrong in some way. I'd be unable to walk through the doors of a cafe or get overwhelmed in Sainsbury's and come back feeling tragic. I bought a bright blue raincoat from a vintage shop in the city centre. On the way home I started to understand that it was a very ugly blue raincoat. It began to rain heavily. I put on the coat and it soaked right through.

 Kips and I had ended things before I left but we were both terribly lonely so we wrote to each other online every night. He sent me movies to watch and songs to listen to. In the evenings I'd make some sad dinner for one. A cup of soup or something on toast, settle in my bed, open my computer, and message Kips. Dark days and nights, with the lamp on. Light, funny chats with someone who wasn't my boyfriend, on a web browser. If our conversations ever got too emotional he'd sign off to watch Italian rugby matches on his browser instead. It seems silly now to think that he never visited – that he never offered and I never asked. I knew that I loved the green dot by his face in the evenings but I wasn't sure of the feeling I'd actually have if he walked in the door. I imagined him standing in my tiny room and looking really old. But really, I was nineteen and he was twenty-two. So young, so what were we scared of?

In November I caught a bad flu. After a week in bed I got over the illness but was left with completely blocked-up ears. It was as if I had dived too deep, got water trapped in my ears and now my experience of life was underwater. But I hadn't dived into anything of course, not life and especially not a swimming pool.

If I was weird when I could hear I was much weirder when I couldn't, particularly as my ears were the most blocked up in the mornings when most of my lectures were. Sometimes it helped to pull both earlobes down so that the canals opened a bit but, even then, I couldn't hear most of what the lecturer was saying. Even seminars were difficult. I was terrified of being called out having not heard the question. I worried that if I did talk, I would be talking too loud. So instead I spoke very quietly. I couldn't hear myself and nor could others. Basically, I tried to make myself invisible and talk to no one so all chance of embarrassment could be avoided.

Abs visited for the weekend and, noticing how odd I had become, convinced me to book an appointment with a doctor. When she left and I finally made the miserable walk, through the grey drizzle, down a mile of student housing to the back of the big Sainsbury's, the doctor told me there was too much wax in my ears to see whatever was going on in there anyway. She said I was going to have to put olive oil in my ears for several weeks before she could look at it.

At the pharmacy I gave them my prescription, paid seven pounds and was handed a tiny glass bottle of olive oil and a pipette in a paper bag. The sticker said: *Use twice daily for one month*. On the walk back to my halls, the rain picked up and came through my non-waterproof raincoat. I felt very vague. Vaguely, I was disappearing and the rain was just slowly, half-heartedly washing me away. I had no personality, no opinions, no beliefs. It didn't matter if I was here or not. I was existing but also not really. I was able to have conversations but not really. The only other people I saw on the pavement were students on their way to Sainsbury's or students returning from Sainsbury's, with heavy orange bags.

I got to my room, closed the curtains and turned a lamp on. My skin, my clothes, my hair, it was all unfortunately still there and also soaked. I changed into my PJs, lay on the bed, sucked some of the tiny olive oil bottle up with the pipette and squeezed a few drops in one ear. Cold oil oozed in, tickled my ears and filled them up even more.

After a week of the olive oil I couldn't hear a thing morning to night, even when I pulled my lobes down. Soon, both ears became infected. I couldn't face going back to that doctor. Without packing or thinking about it too hard I put on my shit raincoat one morning and took a bus to the train station to go home.

That week my dad really looked after me. He booked me another appointment with a doctor, picked up the antibiotics, brought up soups and teas and then the pills at exactly the minute I was meant to have them. He drove to the video shop in town and rented a pile of DVDs that had something to do with the Cold War lectures I was missing.

No more fleas, but lying on my mattress in the middle of *Dr Strangelove*, I felt a slight tickling movement coming out my right ear. A quickening trickling and then a serious trickling when the wax and olive oil and god knows what else flowed out. Soon the left ear was emptying too. It was really one of the most disgusting things that has ever happened to me, but also one of the most satisfying. All that wax and trapped water and misery that had been blocked in my head for the past month, loosened to brown stinking gunk. I got up from the mattress, stuck some tissues in my ears and ran downstairs to find my dad. When I told him I could hear again he jumped out of his chair at the kitchen table and hugged me, so relieved.

I quickly realised it wasn't just that I could hear again but that I could hear everything and beyond. My dad put the kettle on and the whole kitchen roared to a boil. The fibres of my T-shirt were a bag of snakes. My father's voice was pots falling out of a cupboard. Up in my room I sat down at my desk and opened a book. I could hear the pages turn in my teeth.

When I went back to Manchester the intensity of sounds wore down, though something remained. Saliva clicking against people's tongues as they spoke. A tinny snakiness to the wrong sounds. Walking down the Oxford Road on the way to a lecture, a leaf fell from a tree behind me. I could hear it crinkle and hiss and the sound followed me across the street and all the way into my lecture hall.

I made my first real friend around then. His name was Sam and he was in one of my history classes. It turned out he lived in the tower block that my window looked out on. He was smart and kind and had a habit of dropping whatever he held in his hands. For that reason he will always be linked in my mind to the racket of crashing objects. When I told him about my newfound hearing he laughed and his wallet slipped like a cartoon stick of butter, making a great splash on the ground.

I woke up one night in that breeze-block room, paralysed. It was the same room but something about it was inside out and I couldn't move. Loose shadows came in and out of the door, sliding, never quite taking shape. I couldn't scream or move. A weight pinned me down and I could only watch the shadow ghosts forming and unravelling in the doorway. I knew somewhere beneath the covers I must have hands and arms and legs and fingers. I tried to imagine them back to existence, but they were gone. After what felt like a lifetime, I woke up from the dream-nightmare room again with a start into my regular-nightmare room with a pounding heart, sure that I had finally gone mad.

I invited Sam over the next night to watch a film. He chose a film about French monks in Algeria called *Of Gods and Men* and we watched it sitting up with our legs horizontal on my bed. In the middle of the film my dad called. He told me my cat Pongo had died. He said that Pongo had spent the day sleeping on his knee and he'd then found a corner upstairs. My dad sounded like he'd been crying. I was moved. My cat Pongo. My cat that always ran away from me and was never my best friend and would not be held but died on my dad's leg. Lonely Dad, all his children moved away now. It was just him and Pongo left in the house when my mother was away for work and now it was just him, depressed and trying not to drink.

I couldn't explain that to Sam. Instead we spoke abstractly about the loss of childhood innocence, the death of pets, how it was strange when you didn't know what to feel . . . and then we went back to the monks. At some point I just lay down and closed my eyes. I was afraid of my room and I wanted to go to sleep with someone sitting there. Sam lay down next to me and I turned over to face the wall. The footsteps of French monks echoed through Algerian courtyards and we spent the night like that, on top of the covers in all our clothes. After he left, I stuck a passport photo I had of Kips above my desk and made up that he was my boyfriend. Real or not real, it felt good to have a boyfriend, to say to people that I had someone back home, and unbeknownst to the 3D Kips, he watched over me for the rest of that grim first year – the rest of which I barely remember. There are moments in the past that are clearer to me than the present, and months and years that have just gone rotten. Which is actually what that depressing Manchester room makes me think of because I never washed my sheets. Not once for the whole year. I have never been so homesick. All I wanted was to be back in my room, with the fleas jumping jumping.

Barbecue Bible

When summer came to Ohio, my dad said you could smell the smoke and char of hamburger meat and frankfurters up and down the street all day long. This might have been an exaggeration but it was certainly something he tried to recreate in his own manic way because the first bright, warm day of the year sent him reeling. Stomping, barking orders and driving everyone in our house insane. Out came the extension cord, the CD player looping frantic jazz. The grill, the ancient lawn mower, the giant bag of seeds for the bird feeder. He pulled another huge cookbook, *The Barbecue! Bible*, down from the shelf and left it at the head of the kitchen table, forbidding anyone to move it.

    Hamburgers, carnitas, lamb kebabs, more hamburgers. Potato salad with celery and mustard. Spicy lamb kebabs with blackened peppers, onions and aubergine. The food was always delicious but he was not fun to be around. Pointing, jabbing, ordering, swearing, smoking – the climbing mania that was sure to crash badly as soon as the nice weather went away. That giant barbecue cookbook had a looming, threatening presence on the kitchen table during these smoky afternoons. When the rain came back and my dad became depressed again, one of us would have to quietly return the monster to the shelf.

The summer I returned from my first year at university was a gloomy one. The year without any kids in the house had been brutal for my father. He'd begun to sneak drinks, even with my mother in the house. It was clear to us, when we came back, that his hold was slipping. It scared him, my mother told us. He was losing his grip on the things that had kept him afloat most of his life.

In August, the sun finally came out and after weeks of depression, my father woke up too. He brought his beloved barbecue cookbook down from the shelf, planned a Sunday meal and told Kimber and Rachel they had to come. He was going to make steak tacos, with guacamole, spicy charred onions and home-made salsa. He said it was very important – he wanted all his children to be there.

Kimber came down for the weekend but made it very clear he needed to leave on Sunday at four p.m. to make his train back. Rachel arrived that day at noon. We all sat in the garden and watched our dad mow the grass, plant bulbs, stomp around and do everything but prepare for the barbecue. By three p.m. there was still no sign of lunch, just Dad in the kitchen, banging and swearing and shouting at my mother. Pandora agreed to go help him finish it.

'No, you don't slice it like that, you slice it like this!' we heard him say.

'Whaaat!' Pandora said.

'I SAID YOU DON'T SLICE IT LIKE THAT, YOU SLICE IT LIKE THIS!'

'No, Dad, I didn't mean "what" as in a question, I meant "what" as in "whaaaaat!"'

He stormed out to the top of the garden past us to smoke and fix a bird feeder.

'He's completely insane,' Kimber said to my mother.

'He's just been really looking forward to this barbecue,' my mother replied. Kimber put his head in his hands.

Kimber missed his train of course. We ate in a tense rush, fingers clenched around our delicious tacos, and made faces at each other while Dad chattered on. But he didn't notice at all. He went on and on, grinning with a mouth full of food. 'All my children together!' he kept saying. 'All my children! For ten years it never happened. Can you imagine? And now you're all here? And you might be a bunch of assholes, but goddamn it I love you. I love you all so so much!'

There's a photo that my mum took at the end. We are sat around the garden table. My dad in the middle, bending behind the umbrella pole, his four children around him. There are empty plates, and our expressions are strained and exhausted, but my dad has a wide, sly smile and is reaching one hand behind Kimber's head, making bunny ears.

Sausage Pasta

Of all the meals my dad made, the one that we loved the most, the one that helped us forgive him the fastest, was sausage pasta. A spicy, creamy ragù, with tomatoes, rosemary, wine and Cumberland sausages. He had adapted it from a River Cafe recipe, but now it was his. First, he sautéed onions on low heat. While the onions cooked, he measured the herbs with teaspoons and laid them in a line on a wooden chopping board: a mound of red chilli flakes; a bigger mound of fresh, chopped rosemary from the garden; a tiny pile of flaked salt; and three whole bay leaves. When the onions were ready, he crumbled in the sausages and added the wine and herbs, turning up the heat just enough to brown them slightly. Then he emptied in four cans of chopped tomatoes and cooked the sauce down for a few hours. Before serving, he melted in Parmesan and double cream.

Sausage pasta was for Sundays or birthdays. It was for after a relapse, when he wanted to win us back. Or for when any of my brothers and sisters came to stay. It was a meal to say Well Done, or Don't Worry. Welcome Back, or So Long. Sorry, or I Love You. He always made double, and we always ate it all. I would be shocked at the amount my older siblings could consume. Three, four, five extra helpings. We finished the last of it from the pot with our fingers, hands batting against one another to get that last rich crumb of sausage, and my dad watching, so pleased. However frustrating or depressed he had been that day, we were always happy over a bowl of his pasta. My own friends would invite themselves for dinner if they knew he was making it. It was the one thing that you could rely on, his biggest achievement. If his ladder back from the moon led to the kitchen table, it was made from sausage pasta.

A week before my twenty-first birthday at the start of September, my dad relapsed badly. It happened on a normal day, when we were all in the house. He bought a bottle of vodka from the village Londis, took it up to his office, closed the door and went to bed on the futon. My mother had stern words with him in time for him to recover for my birthday but I was very upset. It was my last week at home. I was going to California for the year as I'd got into an exchange programme. A year seemed like a very long time. My sister was going back to university too, and my mother back to work. Soon, he would be completely alone in the house again.

The night before I left, my dad cooked up a Goodbye sausage pasta. Which was also a Sorry and Happy Birthday sausage pasta. I was hungover myself and anxious about leaving. My parents and Pandora and I sat around the table together and tried to savour the meal. It felt like an important moment, like one of us would say something meaningful that we all needed to hear, and he would realise what he was living for, and it would change everything. But I was tired and had a headache. We hardly spoke, shovelling pasta into our mouths instead. The tears, when they came, started streaming down my face, and my dad looked over at me, like he knew what I was thinking, and said, 'Sweetheart, why are you crying?'

Santa Cruz

I overpacked for California. I had to take out the heaviest things I'd stuffed in my suitcase and balance them in my dad's arms: history textbooks, jumpers and shoes I hadn't worn in years, a big glass pot of pencils and pens. I didn't know how to pack for a year or how to say goodbye to my dad, who would be going back to an empty house alone. I left him at the check-in holding on to my rejected belongings with so much left unsaid and then I cried all the way to San Francisco, until the border agent at immigration warned me to stay away from all the hippies in Santa Cruz, and my new life began.

A train to San Jose. A bus full of crazies, down a winding mountain highway. 'Ocean and Water' announced the automated voice of a fine American lady when we arrived at the first cross-street bus stop downtown. Tanned bums were smoking weed at the station. The bus driver had a glint in his eye. 'Pacific and Spruce' called the same automated voice. 'Bay and California . . . Bay and Seaside . . .' as the bus drove down pretty sun-drenched streets and along the coast. I saw surfers bobbing in the Pacific. Along the railings were surfer graves with crosses and flowers. A handsome young man ran out of his seaside ranch house, letting the door swing. He rode off on his bike with hands held around his back and we carried on up the steep, forested hill to campus, where the university emerged in concrete buildings between the trees.

The campus was a hilltop paradise of golden light and green shadow. My new room-mate Rebecca was golden and shadowy too. We got settled into our room and our new life as easily and breezily as if we had already known each other for years. She came from Pleasant Hill, a suburb across the bay from San Francisco. I imagined a sweet, humble town with palm trees, a little square and a clock tower. From her bedroom looking over the unrelentingly bright lawn she dreamed of rainy streets and grand brick buildings and basements. She'd spent her first two years of college majoring in History and Philosophy at a drizzly university in Oregon before having to transfer here when the folding of her dad's real-estate business meant that her family could no longer afford the out-of-state tuition. Full of Kierkegaard and Catholic guilt and ideas about morality and responsibility, she arrived in Santa Cruz to be put in a room with sun-drunk English me. She was unlike anyone I'd ever met, but for whatever opposites or harmonies or equations went into it, we spoke the same language and felt at home with each other, happy to spend most of our sleeping and waking lives together.

Sun-bleached concrete quads and redwood groves and bridges over ravines. Ocean-view classrooms and ocean-view dining halls. Tater tots and pizza pasta salad and Rebecca. She ate muffins with a knife and fork because she had a fear of sticky hands. She was also afraid of fruit, particularly berries, and the pale and looming sun at noon. She liked the dark, particularly the basement of the Engineering School library, where she went to hide and get her work done. It wasn't that she hated the sun — she just didn't think she deserved to enjoy it yet. I thought that was silly. The point was to live now. 'The dizzying crest,' she said, quoting Camus with equal amounts of seriousness and embarrassment. 'Being aware of one's life, one's revolt, one's freedom, and to the maximum, is living, and to the maximum.'

The leaves that never fell. The sun that always rose. The mornings that began with the song from Rebecca's alarm — washed-out voices recalling suburbs and mountains beyond mountains. The breeze through the open dorm window, the eucalyptus trees planted in the days of John Steinbeck. The dappled path on the way to classes on *Moby-Dick*, the stag that blocked my way, the too many mini muffins from the dining hall's unlimited buffet. The students with their awkward jeans and sweatshirts and enormous backpacks. Rebecca with her outdoors-wear and socks in sandals and existential panic whenever I suggested we cycle to the beach in the middle of the day. Even she couldn't fight the wind that blew us down the hill and the hill that blew us to the ocean, which Ishmael called the 'ungraspable phantom of life . . . The key to it all.'

But where were the hippies? Where were the surfers? Where was the love of my life running out of his beach shack, leaving the door swinging? We walked to class, we read in the sun, we spoke in riddles and worried if we were ever going to make any other friends. At a bar in town Rebecca ordered a Tanqueray and tonic because that was what Don Draper drank and she held it in the palm of her hand like Don Draper too. She was not really a girl and not really a boy. She was an old man thinking in a basement at the outbreak of a Prussian war. And she was also just a guilty young thing from Pleasant Hill, California, who had never left the continent and didn't know how good she had it. The beach is not frivolous, Rebecca! The ocean is the truth . . . The ungraspable phantom of life! Yes, yes, yes, of course, she agreed. I've got problems and I need your help!

On Halloween I dressed as a Hogwarts student and she dressed as Darth Vader and we met Jack the Sars patient and Michael the Nerd. Jack and Michael were best friends. Michael was wide-eyed and Jack was sly-eyed. They were both feral and naive and bold as cartoon characters. Michael stood an inch away from Rebecca's face when she was talking. An attempt to kiss her? It was unclear. But then when nothing happened he ran away. Jack threw a plastic cup at a big guy and then pretended it was someone else. Michael came back with lipstick smeared across his mouth from kissing a dancer called Megan, and when Rebecca informed him of this he screamed and ran away again . . . this was how we all became friends.

Michael had a 1971 VW bus that he'd been sleeping in because his room-mate had taken to sitting on the edge of his bed in the middle of the night. Jack had dreams of apps and comedy and inventions and writing plays but most importantly he had dreams. There was also Pero, a dog-like boy who wanted to be a firefighter, and a gentle boy called Dibs who liked sweet things and played the saxophone, and Jessie, who was like an older sister Wendy to these lost boys. Michael drove his old bus like someone who knew for certain he wasn't going to die yet. We packed into the van and picked up random people along the way, and when the brakes failed at the foot of the hill and we rocketed through a red light with a song blaring, I did not believe I was going to die yet either.

California, the golden land of open doors and open faces and open windows and van doors that blew open when Michael was driving. All these young people with ugly shoes and guitars and big ideas and dreams. I didn't want to sleep or dream. I wanted to soak up every drop of California while I had it right out the window, with Rebecca in the dining hall, Rebecca in the dorm room, Rebecca and me cycling to the beach in the golden hour to watch the sun go down. Rebecca bringing me peace and consistency and dizzying snatches of philosophy, and waking us up every morning with her song about suburbs and mountains and a flask of tea.

And how was she to know that the one morning she'd sneak out early to go finish an essay in the Engineering School's signal-less basement would be the morning that a girl from the student office knocked on the door with news that I needed to call my mom. I bought credit on Skype and my mother answered. 'What do you want me to say, Helen? How can I say it? What can I say?' She managed eventually to tell me that she'd come home to find my dad collapsed and maybe he'd fallen or maybe it was a stroke but his brain had died and I needed to get home as soon as I could if I wanted to say goodbye. I couldn't get hold of Rebecca in the signal-less basement, but I found a girl on my floor with a car who could drive me to the airport. And how was that the first day of rain I'd ever seen in California? Terrifying sheets of rain that turned the winding mountain highway into a silver river and took my tears away for the rest of the long journey home.

At the hospital his forehead was still warm and his hands were still warm and seemed to be just like his regular living hands when the nurse turned off the machine. At home his slippers were beside the shoe basket, his jacket on the coat hanger, his briefcase by the record player. There was a full bowl of Halloween candy still by the door and all the makings for sausage pasta out on the counter. We cleaned up the house and ate the candy and cooked the pasta and planned the funeral and followed the coffin hand in hand. And was it the night before or the night after that a mystery one-eyed matted ginger cat that none of us had ever seen came in through the cat flap and curled up in the corner of the kitchen to begin the process of dying around all the hustle and bustle, only to vanish as if we had imagined it?

I packed all the things I'd left in my dad's arms the first time around and somehow found more things I didn't need so that at the airport my suitcase was too heavy again. But this time, the check-in agent took pity, accepted the suitcase and waved me on.

PART TWO

Window to a Room

Poetics 2

I woke up to a fresh glass of water and a tea gone cold. There was a bowl of muesli on the kitchen counter, also left for me by George before a kiss upon the forehead and he went to work in central London. The dishes for Yazzie's fried-egg breakfast in the sink. The dishes for Abs's cereal washed and dried on the side. No dishes for Pandora because she must have left for work in a hungover rush after Wine and Whine Wednesdays. All I had to do was pour milk into the bowl, make a hot tea and try to get out. But the morning was gloomy, and our cheerful but damp home was only damp without other people in it. I had two showers, got dressed and undressed a few times, got in and out of bed, made and remade the bed, did the dishes, swept the floor, mopped the floor, made a shopping list, hid in the bathroom when the postman knocked and at some point by the end of this wasted day – another day on top of what was now a five-year collection of cosy and sweet and maddening days in this house with my sister, my boyfriend and my two best friends – my old California friend Jack called with a proposition. He was putting on a play in San Francisco – some kind of comedy featuring Aristotle's lost poetics, two classicists, two monks and five cancelled comedians. He wanted me to fly out for a month to play one of the classicists. He'd already cast all the other roles, including the other classicist, who was going to be Michael.

'Oh no!' I said. 'That will be a nightmare. Can't he be a monk instead?'

'It will be perfect, don't worry,' Jack said. 'You can be the voice of reason. And anyway . . . he's on the up.'

My sister and my oldest friends came back from work, leaving muddy footprints along the hallway, apart from George who diligently took his shoes off when he came in the door. I told them about Jack's crazy invitation. 'You have to go,' Yazzie said, while I got down on my hands and knees to mop up her muddy prints. 'You need to get out of this house.' Even George agreed. Though later, when the two of us went to bed, he asked me: 'But what if you don't come back?'

It was only when I landed in Oakland one month later and walked through the sunny little airport, passing a man with long grey hair playing 'Surfin' USA', that I realised I wouldn't be able to go back. Jack picked me up in his rusty Subaru and dragged me straight to a jam session, then to a beautiful Berkeley supermarket and then to his messy room in a shared house, where it turned out I would have to avoid his housemates as much as possible, because they weren't happy with the prospect of me staying there for a month. He had only told them yesterday. 'Are you joking?' I said. 'Don't worry,' he assured me. The window by his bed was always open so I could come and go through there. There was a mattress set up on his filthy floor for me to sleep. I didn't even mind about the window, or that the floor was so filthy and that there were dirty bowls and spoons of crusted yogurt all over the place.

'It's too nice to not wake up alone,' Jack said in the morning.

'It's too nice to wake up in California,' I said from the stinky mattress across the room.

And it was too easy to forget my home in London because by the time we set off for the city the next afternoon, my other country was already asleep and we were driving across the Bay Bridge with the windows down to meet with the rest of the cast for the first table read at Cameron and Teddy's apartment in the Mission. All the cast was there except Michael, including a few old college friends I hadn't seen in years. An hour later, there was still no sign of him, and no way of reaching him. We all knew he had no phone. Jack was ready to call the whole thing off: 'He's not a person any more. He will always disappoint me.'

At eight p.m. news came from Michael's new girlfriend that she'd driven him from Santa Cruz to San Jose and dropped him off at the train station. At nine p.m. the buzzer went. Everyone apart from Jack went to the door to listen to him climb the stairs. Big hugs, a big welcome for Michael! He was tanned and bedraggled, in a hideous pink camo puffer jacket with a bandana tied around a sun-bleached mop. A burst of light came in with him . . . you couldn't deny it. You couldn't deny he was very smug about it too. He shook my hand and I felt a jolt.

'What the hell is this jacket,' I said.

He sat down next to me and whipped it off. 'I found it on the street!'

He smelled like washing powder, and that surprised me. I was even more surprised that this was Michael. Goofy, infuriating, impossible Michael. He'd spent five years in the Santa Cruz Mountains, not graduating, living off other people's acid and vegetables, and it looked good on him.

Jack handed him the script. 'OK, gang,' he said. 'Let's just read it all the way through. Don't worry about the acting yet.'

So we read our lines. The play was smart and difficult to follow and I felt silly, just reading my lines sat around a coffee table with long-lost friends and a few random comedians. When it was all over, I went out on the balcony for a cigarette. Michael followed after me and asked for one too.

'What's been the most important thing in your life in the last five years?' he asked.

'Love,' I said and instantly thought that sounded foolish. I suppose I was thinking of George, who I loved dearly and who loved me, and my sister and my two best friends and the pocket of semi-adult shared-living home life that we'd built over the last five years, which held my life together so tightly it was making me a nervous wreck.

'I dunno, actually,' I said. 'I don't know why I said "love".'

He laughed with his eyes or it seemed like a laugh. It was the same slapped wide-eyed vaguely smiling Buddha face he'd had in college. The face that confused people and made them notice him and want him to be around them and wonder where he was when he wasn't around. People were always asking: 'Where's Michael?' His whole manner had unnerved and repelled me back then but now he was just standing there and so was I.

'Don't laugh at me,' I said. But that's not what I meant. It was the first time I noticed that his big brown eyes had flecks of gold in them. Brown water with spots of sun. Fire and brimstone in the water too. I also noticed that his bandana was decorated with Halloween pumpkins.

Well, I asked him. What was the most important thing in *his* life?

'My art,' he said, laughing hysterically when I grimaced. 'But it's the only thing that lasts. Everything else is insatiable. When I wake up, I think what can my free mind do before I feel hungry, horny or tired. I have to get there before they get me. Because if I'm not making I'm consuming and if I'm consuming than I'm never full and if I'm never full then I'm empty and I'm dead!'

Well, if I was foolish, he was self-obsessed and scrambled from taking too many drugs. We finished our cigarettes and went inside. Not long after, Jack and I drove back to Oakland. We would all reunite tomorrow for rehearsals.

'Is Michael an idiot or a genius?' I asked Jack from my little mattress in the corner.

'He's a fucking idiot,' Jack said. 'He thinks he's better than everyone. He's deluded. He's completely incapable of getting it together and making something of himself. I can't be friends with him any more. It's too disappointing. I just have to suck it up for this play and that will be it. You have no idea.'

But in the morning, with the window open, my personal door to California, bringing in birdsong and sunlight and a new day, Jack changed his tune.

'He's also a genius. He's a mixed-up genius. He lives one foot in a character. He's the funniest person I know. He's a true artist. The magic shines out of him and he wiggles into incredible situations. People love him in a way that they don't love me.'

By the afternoon, Jack was bitterly disappointed again. Michael had returned to Santa Cruz, missing the next day's rehearsal. Jack had the idea that I should call Michael on his girlfriend's phone and act interested, like I really really wanted him to come back. It was the only way to guarantee that he would return and not destroy the play. When he did return at the end of the week, Jack sent the two of us out walking, with strict instructions not to come back until Michael had learned his lines. Nothing was sticking, but Michael wasn't worried. He had burned out the part of his brain that worried. 'If you've taken acid a hundred times,' he asked us, 'aren't you always on acid?' And that was how I found myself spending so many strange and magical days wandering around San Francisco with just Michael. We jumped the BART, met some freaks in a hacker's space, climbed up and down hills and took the old tram down to the bay. He'd steal supermarket sandwiches and I'd buy us a few beers in the evening, which we would drink on the stoops of fancy houses and watch the sun go down, before heading back to rehearse with Jack in the evening. I slept on my mattress in the corner of the dirty room and the two of them slept in Jack's bed. When I spoke to George on the phone, I had already become a stranger. I couldn't remember the girl who had left. I felt like a boy and a monstrous one at that. The three of us were coming and going through Jack's window. We read to each other at night. Once Jack read a story in which a robot told a lovesick man that everything in life was finite apart from love, which was infinite. We played a bedtime story game, where one person would say a word and another would tell a story from it. When I said 'dog', Michael told a story about a woman called Miss Betty and her golden retriever. They lived opposite him growing up and the dog walked everywhere Miss Betty went, always with a little lead in its mouth. One night, Michael told us, the house caught fire and the dog woke up Miss Betty, saved her and probably saved the next house from burning down too. Michael's mom woke him up in the middle of the night and took him over to the kitchen window to show him the burning house. And there was the golden retriever, watching the flames with the little lead in its mouth!

On another night, Michael gave the word 'rabbit' and I told a story about the time my dad bought me a rabbit when I was nine, to make up for his drinking. Actually what my dad asked was: 'Would you rather have a boyfriend or a rabbit?' Who knows why those were the two options. He was drunk. But at the end of the summer there was a rabbit in a green hutch at the back of the garden that nobody wanted. There was something wrong with that rabbit. It couldn't run in a forward direction, only in circles. When you let it out of the hutch it would go loop-de-loop while making frightening squealing noises. I'd forget to feed it or clean out the hutch and a month in, after Fireworks Night, the rabbit died.

'I was so upset when I found out – not because the rabbit was dead but because I believed I had killed the rabbit because I'd never wanted it: I'd wanted a boyfriend.'

Jack sighed or was it more of a growl? He threw a blanket over his head and turned himself against the window.

'Alien,' I said to Michael, across the room in the

dark. Whispering, he told me about the time his mom saw a moving light in the sky and called him out to the back yard to watch. They pulled out two deckchairs and watched the UFO make circles in the stars for hours.

'They live among us,' he said. 'They have for millennia.'

When there were just a few nights left before the play, my little mattress had to go to PianoFight, our basement theatre, ready to cushion a falling monk in Act Three. It was the three of us together now in the bed by the window. Jack got in the middle. He said he was putting up with this bullshit for the sake of the play but he was gunna be in the middle every night and it was his turn to tell a bullshit story. So Michael said 'gay horse' and Jack told a story about a sexually frustrated gay horse called Michael who fucked another gay horse called Michael and made a donkey called Mike. The two of them started to fight. Michael tried to get in the middle.

'No!' Jack said. 'It's wrong. Helen, you were supposed to be on my side. You were supposed to be the voice of reason. Wherever you two are going with this . . . turn around. It will be a disaster.'

The next night, needing to escape the irate director, I followed Michael down the rabbit hole to a house full of fried acid heads on the outskirts of the city. Writing on the walls, cushions on the ceiling, and a guy called Trippy Chris in the basement, playing an abrasive beat on a loop. The room we were in belonged to a guy called Bob, who was eloping to Reno that night, to marry someone who was also, implausibly, from Bath.

The night after that, we stayed at Cameron and Teddy's apartment in the Mission. The first performance was tomorrow, not that I was thinking about that at all.

'Breakfast,' I said. I was on the couch and Michael was lying on cushions just beneath.

'Breakfast,' Michael said. 'How about that day you made me and Jack that lovely breakfast?'

'That wasn't lovely,' I said.

'Yes, I know,' he agreed. 'You told me to make the tea and I got distracted with my music and forgot.'

'Yes,' I said. 'And when you forgot to make the tea, that was when I saw our whole future. Me asking you to do things and you sweetly not doing them. And everything in my own creative life coming second to yours and you completely eclipsing me.'

'I'll never do that again,' he said. 'Or I probably will. But I'll try not to.'

I didn't want to go to sleep so I gave another word. 'Pie.'

'When I think about pie,' he said, 'I imagine our future. During the day you go to your world and I go to my other world. Then we meet at the diner between our two planets in the evening and share our slices of pie.'

We slept together for the first time that night and I accepted that I loved him. The train had left the station, flown off the rails and there was nothing I could do about it, and neither could Jack. 'He's completely pulled you into the muck,' Jack said. Well, I couldn't see anything else, or any way back. An hour before the first performance I drank from Michael's Gatorade water bottle, not realising he had dropped a tab of acid inside. On the stage, he saw all of his lines written in spinning orbs above the audience. He would pick one at random. I remembered all my lines and all of his lines and was temporarily blinded by the stage lights. Three weeks later, the hallucination had not ended. Had there been acid in every water bottle? 'Well now you know how your father felt,' my mother had said. 'Deceiving the people he loved . . . It completely tore him apart.' A small room became free in Cameron and Teddy's apartment and Michael and I took it. I only had a duffel bag of belongings but Michael filled the room with his music equipment and stuck papers covered in notes and song lyrics across the walls. There was now another mattress pressed up to the floor-length window in the corner which we covered in a flaming orange quilt. We didn't have curtains or blinds, so in the morning the sun woke us up, hit the flaming quilt and turned the white walls of our room orange. There was no need for the bedtime stories any more because we had our own ruined breakfasts, UFO sightings, slices of pie and all-night arguments. But now and then, particularly in our most lovely and terrible moments, I'd be hit with a strange pain in the knowledge that what we were living so vividly could not last, that one day it would end and become a story. A story like a quilt – a stinky old orange quilt on a single mattress pressed up against a window, where the sun bounced from the bed to the walls and for the first moments of the day I clung to him with such happiness in a room that looked like it was burning.

Days of Roses

In the Rose Garden of Golden Gate Park with a six-pack of Little Sumpin' because it's Michael's favourite beer. Seven point five per cent and ten dollars a pop.

'No! Because of the name. And the little lady on the front. And her sexy leg.'

Oh well. Wandering over to the blossom trees . . . stumbling to the last patch of sun . . . sun on faces, necks on cheeks, hearts on necks.

'You're glowing!' he said. It did feel like it. It did feel like a sparkling vision I had found myself in. A scene someone might dream up who had never been to California, sitting on a rainy bus, listening to The Mamas and the Papas.

Until the sun disappeared and we got on the wrong side of the Little Sumpin'. Walking out of the park he launched his tirade against writing. He said that everything written after 9/11 was useless now. Books were dead. People who still read them were tools. I shouldn't take offence, though. This was just a version of the truth. His words, blunt tools, might be harsh but he came in peace and if I took offence that was my ego talking and I needed to talk to my ego and get over myself.

'What's wrong with you?' I said. He said he was sorry and snatched a bouquet of lilies from a storefront and handed it to me.

'No, Michael!'

'Oh no. I've offended you again!' He stole a bunch of yellow roses from the next store.

'Stop! No more!'

Walking through The Castro, holding three cloud-coloured lilies in one hand and a bunch of yellow roses in the other. The sky bruising pink to purple. The street streamed with people, wandering out of parks and bars and holes, by the looks of them. A deranged, crazed mood in the air that could make a person think: What am I doing here? What have I done?

We passed a man in a camo jacket opening a fresh pack of mellow yellow American Spirit.

Michael asked if he could bum one. The guy looked between us and all the flowers. He was stocky, with a shaved head, and he swayed like a city tree, lightly in the breeze.

'Sure. No problem, man. Take two.' We thanked him. Michael took a lily out of my hands and offered it to him. The man shook his head, smiled and swayed. He handed us a light. Michael lit the two cigarettes as I took in the street with its rainbows and neon lights and purpling sky. The shopfronts with their bongs and dildos and novelty cookies. The Castro Theatre, flashing red. This place that was radical once and had now become a circus for tourists, the super-rich and the dispossessed.

'How's your night going?' Michael asked him.

'I'm fucking drunk,' the man said. 'I was in Iraq. Killed ten ragheads. You want another cig?'

'No, we're good. Thanks,' I said.

'I'd kill more if I could.'

For some reason Michael offered him the lily again. The man shook the flower away, said, 'Enjoy the night.' He had to go. He was late to meet his boyfriend.

We left him on the street and carried on past the theatre and turned on to Market.

Smoking our cigarettes, neither of us speaking. All I could taste was shame and burning. I swore to myself that after this cigarette I would never smoke another.

'What should we have said? What are you meant to say at a time like that? Why did you give him a flower?'

'To appease the demon.'

We carried on walking in silence. From the silence came a man's screams. Behind the tram a man appeared, a very different man, small and desperate, zigzagging down the middle of Market Street. Cars beeped and swerved around him.

'Hellpffffucking help me!' A car sped up very close to him and he swung himself on to the sidewalk in our direction. 'Help me! I need to go home!' he screamed.

He didn't look homeless. He had clean clothes and a smart backpack, neat haircut and a close shave. But his face, as it got closer, reminded me of an animal caught in a cage. They were not human eyes, jet black with no depth, staring without blinking. They did not look sad. They were very frightened and shivering and that frightened me.

'Where is home?' Michael said. The man let out another great wail and doubled over.

'If I knew that,' he said between heaving breaths, 'you think . . . I would be . . . fucking . . . here?'

'It will pass,' Michael told him. He pulled out a stolen rose from my hand and offered it to the crying man.

'You asshole! You don't fucking know. You fucking asshole. Who the fuck are you. I'll kill you. Kill me now!'

The man squared up to Michael. Their noses almost touched. Michael's cool brown eyes stared the man down.

'It will pass,' Michael said.

'Fuck you. Fucking fuck you.'

'It will pass.'

A line of snot hung thickly from the crying man's nostril and I swear, I swear, Michael was ready to breathe it in. Very carefully, never taking my eyes off the hanging snot, I pulled Michael away.

'Sorry,' I told the man. 'Sorry. It is going to be OK.'

'No!' the man screamed. 'Don't hurt him! He didn't mean to! Don't hurt him. Don't leave him. It's not his fault.'

'I know. I won't.'

'Don't hurt him!'

'I won't.'

'I LOVE YOU!' he shouted to Michael as we backed away further.

'I love you too!' Michael shouted back at him.

'Don't hurt him! Don't hurt him!' the man kept screaming, before returning to his old chant. 'I need to go home. I need to go home . . .' and back to zigzagging down Market Street. The cars beeping and swerving. 'Help me! I need to go home!'

Michael and I held hands and walked back to our room. By this point I was no longer angry. I couldn't remember why I was angry or where in the day or my life or this world it had all gone so wrong. Somewhere between the roses and the Little Sumpin'. Somewhere between being born and finding love and losing love and death coming for us all.

Behind us the lost man got smaller and smaller in that sunset hellscape and, for all we knew, disappeared.

Nipomo

Michael wasn't sleeping. A quarter tab of acid for his breakfast. Spliffs throughout the day, booze and blue raspberry C4 pre-workout all through the night. He was recording an album, working on his set, making a website, building a 24/7 open-source radio livestream at a free hackers' space, not finishing anything. He sold a guitar to make rent but the money was running out and he was refusing to get a part-time job.

I was writing and picking up catering gigs and spending a lot of time crying on the hot roof of the apartment building when Michael wasn't around. He found me up there one afternoon at the end of one of his twelve-hour stints at the hackers' space. Two straw hats, a beer, two cups. 'I know you like to drink out of little cups!' He smiled and the inside of his mouth was blue from the raspberry pre-workout. How do you hate someone as much as you love them? He said he'd been looking for me because he had a great plan. A childhood friend in the city was driving down to their hometown and we could get a ride. I could meet Michael's parents; go to the beach; see the fields, wildflowers and back roads. So beautiful this time of year. I wondered if it might save us. 'It's God's country,' he said.

We arrived at his parents' the following morning, after a four-hour drive south. A low ranch-style house on a wide road of low ranch-style houses. Michael said it was too nice a day to be stuck inside, so he took me around the side and we climbed straight up on to the roof: 'I know you like roofs in California.' I did like roofs in California. The front and back yards of gravel, woodchip and pebbles, interspersed with the occasional palm tree or redwood. At the end of the road was the main street, a couple of stores, a steak house, and a taqueria. Beyond, fields of lemon trees and mustard grass and farmland that stretched a few miles inland, up to a range of golden hills. Somewhere behind us was the ocean and, twenty minutes down the coast, Vandenberg Air Force Base. Above us, the sun shone like the grille of a new truck. And the real trucks below all looked new somehow, even being so close to the dirt of the farms and the fields. One by one they crawled the streets with their teeth bared, sweet neighbours smiling behind the wheel, thinking: God's country. Another beautiful day in paradise. Pesticides in the air, Roundup in the ground. If there's a cloud in the sky it's chemtrails or toxic plumes from the industrial sprayers . . .

I put my head on Michael's chest and thought about

what it might be like to grow up here. The freedom! I felt that if I just rolled off the roof I'd be fine. And that if I really wanted to I could just jump off, bounce along the lemon fields and land in the hills, unscathed. The air was so still and the things that were moving – a bird here, a branch swaying there – seemed to be happening on a loop, like a video game, every few minutes. A thought that must have been Michael's really – like most things in my life at this point.

'Poor girl,' he said, his phrase of the week. 'You're catching on.'

The house was full of knick-knacks and shells and crystals and string lights. A *Be Grateful* sign by the coffee maker. A *Be Grateful* mat by the front door. A canvas in the kitchen printed with a picture of three fluffy ducklings and the words 'I have joy down in the bottom of my heart'. It was hard to make out how many cats there were. And then Poopoo, the overweight chihuahua, waddled in from the hallway and charged at Michael, baring his red gums and gnashing tiny, pointed teeth. Michael told me the dog was the spawn of the devil and the root cause of all the issues that existed between him and his parents. I already knew that the issues between Michael and his family had begun when Michael had gone to college in Santa Cruz five years before, found psychedelics, wouldn't get a real job, and kept having to move back home when he ran out of money.

★

His parents were musicians who'd met in Santa Barbara in the seventies. His father Gene was from Michigan originally but had run away to California when he was twenty-three. His mother was born in New Jersey but had fled with her mother to California when she was a young teen, leaving behind her beloved but alcoholic father. In Santa Barbara, Linda had sung in one band and Gene had played guitar in another. They'd worked in the same hippie jewellery store together downtown before marrying and moving to a smaller town up the coast. I met them that morning when they followed the pets into the kitchen. Gene was short and round with a kind face, freshly shaved with a peaked cap on his bald head and a smart cowboy shirt tucked into chinos. He gave me a warm hug that smelled of Irish Spring. He picked up Poopoo and fed him some bratwurst from the fridge. Linda went straight to the coffeepot. She wore a blue shirt with cropped leggings and had her blonde hair put up neatly in a clip. She had the same unblinking stare as Michael.

Gene left to work his shift at a music shop in the next town over and Linda said she needed more coffee before her pain medication kicked in and she could talk properly. She had arthritis and had pain from a series of botched surgeries. The pain was the worst in the morning, but she was managing it with physical therapy, swimming and half a pill on the bad days. She spent the next hour pacing around the house, telling me about all the things she needed to do – pay the bills, fill out paperwork, physical therapy, feed the dog, feed the cats – only to be derailed from doing any of it by the pets, or the phone ringing. She kept apologising for being so busy, but she couldn't seem to get anything done. The bills stayed untouched in a pile that took up most of the kitchen table, the phone rang and rang. There were Post-its all over the house: *Put coffee out*, *Tell Dad to clean sink*, *Ask Michael where he is living in SF*, *Be Grateful*.

Michael derailed her the most, as he tried to make breakfast and clean up after himself. Mother and son knocked around the place, from the coffeepot to the piano to the back door, to the front door to the coffeepot again. They both had the habit of getting lost mid-action, and the same strange sweetness. At one point, just after getting at him about putting the dishes away in the wrong place, she went into the living room and sang out with joy for no apparent reason. When she came back into the kitchen she was smiling. She put her arms around her son. He rested his cheek on the top of her head and closed his eyes.

Michael and I spent the afternoon walking around town. Not a place built for walking but it had its charm, the slanting golden light making even the Vons supermarket look beautiful. We bought three beers for five dollars at the Stop & Shop and watched the sun go down as we sat against a fence by a dusty abandoned lot. He told me that the most famous thing about Nipomo was

Dorothea Lange's *Migrant Mother* photograph. 'That put Nipomo on the map.' I wanted to know why Nipomo was named Nipomo. Michael couldn't remember. I looked it up on my phone. Nipomo meant 'foot of the hill'. That made sense, we agreed, leaned against each other, watching the purpling humpback hills in the distance. Foot of the hill, crook of the arm, the palm of God's hand, Nipomo.

For dinner Michael made sandwiches and, to his mom's exasperation, moved the bills off the table and told everyone we were going to sit down. They were very good sandwiches, pastrami and banana peppers and mayo with a steak seasoning, on thick slices of bread. He made a sandwich each for his parents, and two types for me and him to share. 'Me and Helen share everything,' he announced. 'We're in love.'

After a few bites, Linda started talking about how hard it was, living with her husband, how she loved him but needed him to leave. 'I keep telling him, but he won't go. He does nothing around the house, just eats and spends and plays his guitars.' When she married him, he was already deep in debt. He'd never told her how bad it was. Then she said to me: 'I love my son, but I'd understand if you wanted to leave him. Don't make the same mistake I made.' Gene didn't say anything in response, just happily ate his sandwich and seemed to be somewhere else. Michael went to the fridge and popped a Corona.

★

The next day was a Saturday. We borrowed Gene's car and spent the day in the ice-plant dunes of Grover Beach. When the sun set, we snuck into a motel jacuzzi. Crouched in the bubbles, Michael said he'd told his dad that he'd marry me if he had a dollar. That made me laugh. 'I don't want your dollar,' I told him. 'I just want you to get a part-time job!'

Gene was in the kitchen when we got back, enjoying a Corona Familiar in a frosted glass. He was in a good mood from playing a gig at a wedding where he'd devoured a seafood-platter buffet. 'I tell you . . . those crabs. All that fish. Mountains of it.' We sat at the counter with him. Over more Coronas, Linda cackling along to *Scrubs* on the TV, he told me about his first love. At one point he made the mistake of asking Michael what his plans were. Michael said he was going to start an open-source 24/7 radio station that spread empathy across the world and freed a billion people. He already knew his mission on Earth, God had told him. His parents didn't need to worry. Gene turned to me with a smirk. 'I told Michael to experiment with LSD. I didn't realise he'd be experimenting so frequently.'

They drove us to the train station in San Luis Obispo the next afternoon. Another sunny day but things felt different. Now I knew that this impossible person had a mother and father who loved him and that he made some kind of sense beside them. When his parents hugged us goodbye his dad whispered something in Michael's ear. 'If I had a dollar,' Michael said. We found a booth with a table in the train's observation car, beside a window. Gene and Linda spotted us as they were driving out of the parking lot and circled back through three or four times, waving as the train left the station. Leaving San Luis Obispo, the train wound around and between the Pacific Coast Ranges. The slopes reached up on either side, rolling above the windows. Michael leaned on my shoulder while I read him a story I'd written about my dad. It made him cry. I told him not to move yet – a girl in another booth was painting a picture of us. I could see it in the corner of my eye, strokes of yellow and green and gold.

Six months later, Gene was diagnosed with stage four cancer. A melanoma that had not been removed properly in the spring had spread to his organs by September. By the time Gene began chemo, Michael and I were living in Chicago, sleeping on a futon at a studio that my sister Emma ran. She had been living in the city for five years with her partner and young son and she was eager for company. She set us up with jobs as studio assistants, prepping and cleaning up after baby showers and photoshoots during the day and after parties and music videos at night.

The family told Michael not to come back yet – it would be more stressful with him there. So we stayed in Chicago for September and into October. Michael's desperate restlessness and acid-fuelled benders had subsided, and our relationship had calmed to a more dependable, if rocky, companionship. We kept our clothes in a cupboard and pretended to the people who rented the space that we didn't live there. When the studio was in use, we visited my sister and her son Max, or wandered around Lincoln Park, or walked along Lake Michigan, waiting for the call from his family to say that he needed to come home. Sometimes Michael brought his guitar and I brought my notebook and we'd have glorious afternoons, playing and writing and messing around, cooling our feet in the lake. Other times we couldn't cope, and would find ourselves stuck in the same spiralling argument walking around the humid parks. He said I was unloving and spiritually dead inside. I said that he was cruel and overbearing and didn't listen and we would never find peace together. That I was too sensitive and he was too hurtful and brash and bullish. And why did he have to say such cruel things? Why did we have to have such terrible arguments every day? Why couldn't we just have a nice day and be happy? To Michael, my doubts only proved how godless and unloving I was. He couldn't admit that he had any role to play or that we had any problems, which only made me doubt the whole thing even more. To him, what was cruel was how little I believed in us. His dad was dying and I wasn't there for him. I had one foot in and one foot out and he could feel it. The only thing that needed to happen was for me to find faith. We were twenty-seven. We could move off the grid, have lots of children and raise chickens. In the midst of these never-ending nonsense fights this sounded like a nightmare to me. But what could we do? His dad was dying and he couldn't go home and we were tangled together – separation was unimaginable. I didn't have an answer or a clear idea of what I wanted or what we should do. I did have one foot that was very much tied to him and another foot wondering about an escape. But what was life without Michael? The world would be drained of its colour. He was the complete centre of all my days, my thoughts and worries. I couldn't let go and he wasn't going to let me if I tried. Whenever we had an especially bad argument, he stormed off to the hot-dog place around the corner from the studio, where the staff were famous for insulting their customers. He made friends with the people who worked there. 'The only real people in this city,' he said. Baby Jesus Ted Bundy was one of the names they called him. While he was gone, I'd miss him. He would come back in the best of moods and we would be happy again.

Our daily dramas were interrupted one evening by a call from his sister. She told him the doctor said it was a matter of days now. He spent his entire savings, four hundred dollars, on a flight for the next morning. I packed up the futon and moved into my sister's apartment. After a week he called to say his dad really was dying now and he needed to see me. Please could I come soon? Emma found me a flight from Chicago to LA for fifty dollars for the next week.

★

The Amtrak train from Los Angeles to San Luis Obispo goes up the Pacific Coast, at times along the beach and at others high in the cliffs. Golden beaches, golden cliffs, golden sun lighting tiny fires on the waves. As we got to the central coast the sun met the ocean, right behind a giant oil rig. It made an ominous silhouette against the setting sun.

Michael was waiting for me on the platform, wearing a black hoodie and a black cap with a small red-and-white mushroom on the front. He called it his mourning costume. In the car he gave me a paper bag. Inside was a bar of chocolate wrapped neatly in tissue paper. He drove out of the lot and a full moon appeared over the trees.

We arrived at the house to find Gene sitting on a red La-Z-Boy, watching *Blazing Saddles*, Poopoo on his lap. The dog jumped off when he saw us coming and charged at Michael's ankles. Michael picked him up, thrashing, and plopped him outside, slamming the screen door. Gene had almost halved in size, his face completely sunken; his arms and legs, bluish and pale, poking out of a baggy T-shirt and shorts. I tried to hide my shock but it must have been apparent. People had been coming over all week to say their goodbyes.

When Michael had first told me they'd put Gene on home hospice, I'd assumed it meant he would be home under regular medical care. What it really meant on his low-cost insurance was a hospital bed in their house, medication, and thirty-minute visits from a nurse twice a week. The rest of the time it was up to Michael, his mother and his sister to look after Gene. Once I arrived, the home hospice had been going on for two weeks and they'd stumbled into a rhythm. Gene slept in the Blue Room (blue walls and carpet), which had once been Michael's bedroom, then the bedroom of a series of lodgers, then a room for Linda to stretch in. Now it was the room where Gene was going to die. There was the hospital bed in the centre and a folding table against one wall, covered in a red paper tablecloth, pieces of hospital equipment, dozens of pill pots and Michael's junk.

Michael and his mother took turns administering a regimen of medication every few hours: liquid morphine, vitamins, blood pressure pills, pills to help his organs deal with all the pills. There was a mattress in the corner covered with a *Lion King* quilt where Michael had been sleeping. Gene had a little bell by his bedside that he rang when he needed something.

I was tired from the travel, so Michael set me up a bed in the Green Room next door. It had green walls, a single bed, another folding table, and a few blankets laid out for the cats to sleep on. Michael gave me his pillow and the *Lion King* duvet and put on another hoodie over the hoodie he was already wearing. We sat down on the bed for a moment and he rested his head on my shoulder. From the next room the little bell rang and he shot up. I got under the covers and drifted off.

The next morning Michael woke me at nine o'clock

with a mug of creamy coffee. 'Get up! We're going to the store!' His dad wanted egg bagels. They'd already given Gene his medicine, taken him for a shower, and rustled up a small first breakfast of eggnog and toast. It was only a quick drive to Vons but Michael drove very slowly, all the windows open, lighting one cigarette after another.

We returned to the sound of the little bell ringing. Gene wanted to sit out on the lounger. He wanted a coffee. Michael helped his dad outside and made the bagels. I did the dishes and Linda put on another pot of coffee while telling me how much pain she was in, her arthritis, her hip – she was falling apart.

I soon discovered that the most demanding part of the home hospice was Gene's appetite. Over the next week we went out three or four times a day to find whatever thing he craved. The bell would ring and Michael would go running. 'My dad wants a steak dinner!' We'd jump into the car to go pick up a steak, then sushi, then burritos. It was moving to witness how dedicated Michael was to doing anything for his dad and there was a cheerfulness to these excursions. Our own problems and differences were far away and driving in the sunshine with a job to do we were united as one.

Linda was paying for these elaborate requests with envelopes of cash she'd saved over the years, each labelled with a particular purpose. Every time she pulled out a new one from the back of a drawer, my heart sank: forty dollars for Michael's birthday, a hundred dollars for a plumbing emergency, a hundred for yard work – all gone.

As the morphine doses got larger and Michael more sleep-deprived, the midnight meals became hallucinatory. Gene would wake up, feel hungry, and ring his bell. Michael would help him into the kitchen and cook whatever Gene instructed. I'd hear all about it in the morning. Clam chowder from a can with packet noodles. Chicken soup with pork gyoza and taquitos. Michael told me that sometimes he'd drift off in the middle of cooking, laying his double-hooded head on the kitchen counter.

'Son!' Gene would say. 'The taquitos are burning!'

I slipped by the Blue Room one morning, sheepishly hoping I could just make a coffee and bring my book out into the back yard.

'Helen! The English Muffin!' Gene called out. 'I want an English pot roast. Can you do that?' I returned to the doorway. Poopoo, who was more or less living on Gene's chest by this point, greeted me with a growl.

'Yes!' I said. 'I think I can.' Waiting for the coffee to brew, I looked up English pot roast. It seemed to be some kind of American idea of an old English stew with potatoes and meat. I couldn't find Michael anywhere.

'Gene . . .' I said, eventually going back into his room. 'What do you mean by English pot roast?'

'I mean Henry the Eighth creamy banquet pot roast. Pig's blood! Potatoes! Lots of meat. Don't forget the meat!'

I called for Michael all over the house, in the front yard, the back yard, down by the shed. Finally a voice came from the sky. 'I'm up here!' he said. I couldn't see him, but some branches moved at the very top of the thirty-foot redwood.

'He wants me to make a medieval pot roast,' I told Michael when he came down. 'I have no idea what the hell that is.'

He laughed. 'Don't worry. I need to give him some more morphine now anyway. He'll go back to sleep and forget all about it.'

Michael was right. He fed his father the liquid morphine, while Poopoo barked and tore at his fingers, and Gene drifted off. Michael took a nap. An hour later the little bell rang again.

'Blueberry pancakes!' I heard. 'Can she do blueberry pancakes?'

Half-asleep, Michael told me there was a pre-mix somewhere in the cupboard, which there wasn't. But I did find flour and butter and milk and blueberries and a recipe for American pancakes. Somehow, every time I put a spoonful of the batter in the frying pan it fell apart into congealed lumps of fat. I washed up the destroyed pancakes, and found a mix for blueberry muffins instead. It was the middle of the day by the time the muffins were done. One came out with a funny face. Two freeze-dried blueberries for wonky eyes and a crease below them like a sideways smile. I thought it looked a bit like Michael. I showed his mother and she agreed. Excited, we woke Michael up with the muffin doppelgänger on a plate.

'Hold it up to your face,' we told him. 'Do your wonky eyes. Smile sideways a bit. See?'

Linda brought a muffin cut up in four with a pile of butter to Gene on a little plate. He put the whole lump of butter on one quarter, had a bite, and dropped the plate down on his lap, exhausted.

'Do you like your muffin, Dad?' Michael said. Gene didn't respond. I felt that in some great way I had failed.

Michael's sister, Bonnie, lived in the next town over. She had a two-year-old girl, Mila, and was heavily pregnant with her second. She'd bring a meal or some shopping over every few days and spend a few hours with her dad. When she and the little girl spilled in through the front door, the whole house seemed to calm.

One afternoon, Gene and Bonnie were stretched out on the sofa, the patio doors letting in a warm breeze. Mila was running around, looking for the cats. Linda was out in the hammock. I was sitting next to Michael on the piano bench. He started playing a peaceful, sweet song. I asked Bonnie what Mila's birth had been like. She said it had been an amazing experience. She said she went full wild woman. At the moment of the birth, she'd been on all fours and felt her whole heart open wide to God. There was no pain, no body, no one else, just her baby and God. Gene said that was the way he felt about death. When the moment came, he was going to go into it with arms open to God. He held his arms out wide as he said it.

Later, Bonnie's husband, Paul, came over. They got out some guitars from the garage, brought them into the Blue Room, and sang songs around Gene's bed. Nineties folk – The Moldy Peaches, Bright Eyes – and then a truly beautiful rendition of 'O Holy Night', Paul on the harmonica, Michael on the guitar, and Bonnie singing. I sat on the mattress and watched them. I wanted them to keep playing together until the end of Gene. 'O night divine, o night . . .'

At the end of the song, Linda came in. She said it was late, Dad was tired, she was tired, we were all tiring him out. Michael said, 'Wow, Mom, you even managed to ruin this.'

Bonnie snapped at Michael, 'Don't talk to her like that.'

Michael said, 'Yeah, yeah, it's all my fault.'

Bonnie's husband asked no one in particular if they'd noticed that the moon's face had changed. 'They've done something to the moon's face,' he said. 'I swear . . .'

'He's tired,' Linda said, turning to Gene. 'Are you tired, sweetie? Tell them you're tired. Michael doesn't believe me.'

'All right, Linda,' Gene closed his eyes. 'I'm tired.'

I followed Michael out to the back yard with a beer and a cigarette and found him up in the redwood again. I coaxed him down with my offerings and convinced him not to climb all the way up the tree in the dark, not tonight.

Gene's body was shutting down. His legs and arms were swelling and leaking fluid. He had to carry paper towels around with him to mop up the mess, but he never complained. We took turns massaging his legs to ease the pain. When it was my turn, I made a bit of conversation, asked him about his life. He didn't want to go into any of that. He just smiled and told me to massage with all the strength my skin and bones could muster.

Amid all this, Michael wanted to have sex whenever he had a minute free. When his dad was sleeping he'd usher me into the Green Room or drive us out to the back-road fields. At night, with the hills behind us, the hum of cars in the distance, a light breeze through the grass, it was kind of spectacular. But it felt forced and I couldn't relax. So often we would go all the way out there for me to freeze over. We'd get back to a new version of our same old argument.

'You're removed,' he told me. 'Checked out. A sandbag.'

'Well, sorry,' I said. 'But I massaged your dying dad's legs earlier. I've come all the way here. I'm doing what I can do. Right now all I can be is a sandbag.'

'I'm exhausted and I need love.'

'We just had sex.'

'Oh yeah. "We just did this, we just did that." Don't talk about the past. I'm talking about right now.'

'I know you're sad but you're being a dick. How can you not see that?'

'I don't want to talk.'

'You were the one who started the conversation. I was just lying here.'

'Exactly.'

The days went on and Gene held on. One evening I noticed a slice of a moon through the kitchen window and realised it had been two weeks since I'd arrived. Despite the pain, Gene still wanted to move around, take a stroll with his walker, barbecue pork, play guitar on the patio with his son.

'This is not how normal hospice patients behave,' Linda said. We were standing in the kitchen, looking at family pictures. In many of them the whole family and some friends were sitting around jamming, having a good time. Not that long ago – five years, maybe.

'Most people just lie in bed. But my husband – he's on his feet demanding fine dining! I don't want to complain, but it makes me think – miracles can happen. And if he does get better, things would have to change around here. There's no money. We can't live like this. Steak-dinner takeout! We'd lose the house.'

I nodded and made to say something, but she carried on. 'Sometimes I think I might be an alien,' she said. 'I'm not like other people. Like lying – people lie so easily but I can never lie. Neither can Michael. We're both like that. I can see how hard it is for him in the world. We just don't make sense here! He needs to get a job, get a car. Get going with his life. You're so good for him. He listens to you. I always told him, if you wanna just do what you want, then find a groupie. You're no groupie. You're like an angel sent here. I mean it. I prayed to God for you and you came. But you've got your life ahead of you. I don't want you to feel like you're trapped.'

Michael must have been listening because he ran out of the Blue Room at that point. He took my hand and peeled me away. 'We're going on a walk now, Mom. She doesn't wanna talk any more.'

'See,' Linda said. 'He'll do anything for you.'

'Love you, Mom!' Michael called as he pulled me out the front door.

'Love you too, son!'

Nipomo in November wasn't too different from Nipomo back in April. Lovely, warm days. Chilly nights. The green-gold hills and fields of mustard grass. In the morning the birds went crazy, sounded like washing machines. When things slowed down, I'd go swing in the hammock, listen to the breeze through the trees or sit out on the concrete patio and have a beer on a lounger. The same lounger that gave Gene the melanoma on his face, which the doctors had not removed properly and had spread so viciously. Those afternoons . . . the sky seemed as solid as the concrete patio I was sitting on. What was death in a town where the afternoons were so beautiful? Where the air was thick with pesticides and the sun could kill you while it brightened your day. Where Linda was only a few bad bills away from losing her house and Gene a few days from losing his life. No wonder Michael didn't trust doctors. No wonder he was incapable of getting a job. Who was I to say what was crazy and what wasn't? That the birds did not have cameras in their eyeballs? That fluoride toothpaste did not affect my pineal gland? Sitting out there on that baking patio, my head was all scrambled and full of pesticides too. I could barely remember my own home, or my family or my thoughts and feelings outside of Michael's family and thoughts and feelings, and I didn't mind it either. There was a strange comfort in losing myself in his life because I suppose then I didn't have to think about my own. I could help Michael care for his father in the last days of his life, something I had not been able to do with my own, and they had welcomed me in as if I had been here all along. It really did seem like I had been here all along too. And while the rest of the family were resting in the day, I could just sit on the lounger in the sun, close my eyes, listen to the real birds and the mechanical spy birds and the wind chimes and slowly cook with the rest of the town. Just the way Gene had told Michael to cook the onions for chicken soup. Slowly . . . slowly . . . make love to the onion!

Finally, a hospice charity found a volunteer to help a bit around the house and keep Gene company. The volunteer happened to be a lady from Essex. She'd moved to Nipomo years ago because her husband worked at Vandenberg Air Force Base. On her first visit, she helped Gene into the La-Z-Boy and I made them tea. She asked Gene who played the piano.
 'Play us one of your songs, Michael,' Gene said.
 Michael was edgy that morning. In a mood that smiled but was one moment away from showing its teeth. He sat down at the piano and began to sing and pound the keys.

> *'We were best friends . . . until you got a chihuahua.*
> *Give Mommy a break! Give Daddy a breakdown!*
> *Give Mommy a break . . . Give Dad a slap in the face!'*

It was a silly song, but the way he sang it was soulful somehow and sad. When he finished, the woman clapped and looked genuinely enthralled. Gene looked incredibly embarrassed.
 'You have a very talented son!' she said to Gene.
 'Yep. Talent has never been the issue.'

Gene was still ringing his bell on his sixty-fifth birthday, the 16th of November, a milestone that had seemed unthinkable a month before. We arranged a small party for his family and a few of his music buddies. Michael spent the morning setting up the back yard with microphones and guitars. He even put a TV and VCR on a cart on wheels to play home videos. We drove to the Mexican supermarket and bought carnitas and a case of mini Corona bottles. On the way out he impulse-bought a ceramic Day of the Dead guitar to give his dad. When the friends arrived at the house, Linda took the opportunity to go have some time alone and run errands at Vons and CVS.

The men barbecued pork, and I made pico de gallo, according to Bonnie's instructions.

It was a hit. The men in their cowboy get-ups were shocked that the English girl had prepared it. The sun was shining, people were sitting out, eating the barbecue. Michael tried his best to get people to play music but it wasn't happening. How do you celebrate the birthday of a dying man? I couldn't figure out what to do with myself. At one point, Michael gave his dad the ceramic guitar wrapped up in Christmas paper. '*Día de los Muertos*,' said his dad. He held the guitar in his palms, disgusted.

The men got it together and started playing some old Western songs and Gene watched on in his wheelchair. They took a break and Michael and I stepped out to catch the sun go down over a field of tomato vines. In the fifteen minutes that we were gone, Gene stood up with a guitar to play a song with them. He was just sitting back down as we came in the door. Soon after, the guys all left.

'Man plans, God laughs,' Michael said.

Linda was gone for most of the day. She returned from her errands with a gift for Michael. She was so excited about it, she wanted to give it to him straight away. Out of a green-and-white paper bag, Michael pulled a fluffy llama with wonky eyes. He squeezed it and the llama squeaked.

'It's a dog toy,' he said, sounding like his father when he held the Day of the Dead guitar. Linda laughed and laughed. She said it reminded her of Michael and the blueberry muffin. I laughed too. Michael grimaced.

'Oh no . . . I think he's angry,' Linda said.

'Here,' I told Michael. 'Don't be angry. Squeeze your dog toy.' He took the llama in both hands, crossed his eyes, stuck his tongue out, and let it rip.

The 18th of November was the seventh anniversary of my own father's death. A long time ago by then but the grief always crept up on me on that date. I woke up feeling totally burned-out exhausted. At this point, I thought to myself, Gene needed to die or someone else would.

I spent the morning swinging in the hammock by the redwood at the bottom of the garden, hiding from everyone. I heard Michael and Linda calling for me from the house. Gene wanted a massage, they said. His legs were hurting. I couldn't face it. Michael called my phone and I ignored it.

When I went back inside, the two of them were manoeuvring Gene into the living room. Michael almost dropped him and he fell back on the sofa with a cry of pain.

'You're not helping!' Linda screamed at Michael.

'Mom. I am mid-helping. You're brain-dead from your painkillers.'

'Enough!' Gene's voice boomed from the sofa, where he was half-collapsed, falling off the side of it. 'Stop it! Both of you!'

Linda and Michael stopped, ashamed.

'Now, son.' Gene took in a quiet, pained breath. 'Can you help me off this damn sofa and take me back to bed.' Michael pulled him up by the armpits.

That night Gene could only manage a spoonful of canned tomato bisque.

'I think he's going to die today. The same date that your dad did. If our dads die on the same day that's God talking. We'll have to get married.'

Later, Michael slept next to me in the Green Room while his mom was with Gene. I dozed while I listened to Linda talk to Gene, telling him about their life together. 'We're good people,' she told him. 'Weird people.' She could have been saying anything really, the hum was so soothing. 'There's no one around here like us.' It kept sending me back to sleep.

I woke up to Gene's voice crying out: 'Help! I can't

breathe!' I pushed Michael and he bolted into the Blue Room. Linda woke up too. 'I'm coming!' she called.

I stayed in bed, listening. They were arguing about how much morphine to give Gene. Linda said Michael was giving him too much. Michael said it wasn't enough. She ran to get the phone to call the nurse. Gene was desperately trying to get words out. He couldn't breathe. And then a desperate gargling, drowning on thin air. Michael was saying, 'It's OK, Dad. I'm right here. I'm right here,' all through the gargling until Gene was no longer making any sound.

When I walked in, Gene's skin had already yellowed, the life just gone. It was five minutes to midnight. An hour later a nurse came. Another hour, and a man and a woman arrived from the mortuary. At the door, their long, grey, thinning hair obscuring half their faces, they told me they were here for the body. Never have I seen more ghoulish-looking people. They wore baggy suits with sleeves that came down over their hands, and round, shiny shoes that also seemed a few sizes too big. They moved so slowly.

'Was he in the military?' they asked.

'No,' we said. 'He was not in the military.'

They put a sheet over Gene's body and wheeled him through the house, out the front door. Linda followed, holding Poopoo. She wanted to show the dog that Dad was leaving. Dad was being wheeled on to the van.

'See, it's OK, Poopoo. There he goes. They're wheeling him in now. He's going . . .'

★

Michael didn't want to watch his dad go into the back of a van. I found him in the yard with a tall glass of vodka, smoking a cigarette. He joked that he'd been praying to his dad as he was dying in the minutes before midnight. 'Come on, five more minutes. If you make it five more minutes it will be the next day and I won't have to marry her.' Then he said that he was plotting to steal morphine to kill the dog.

All the lights were on. It was three in the morning. Michael pulled out a crate of home videos and Linda and I told him to put them away. I made us some tea. We had some more vodka. Linda went to bed and I put Michael in the shower. I washed his hair and cried, but he was like a stone. I could tell he was still obsessing about killing Poopoo.

After the shower, I put him in a clean T-shirt and underwear, tucked him in to bed, and held him tight until he fell asleep. I woke up in the morning to him sleeping soundly next to me. He looked so at peace I didn't want to wake him. It made me cry. His eyes opened. 'Dad?' he said. I couldn't tell if he was joking. Soon after, we heard Linda howling. Long, slow howls. One of the saddest, strangest noises I've ever heard. 'My life!' she called out between the howls. 'My life!' It was almost like singing.

After that first day Linda said she needed to mourn alone. We needed to leave so she could scream and cry and talk to God. We went to Bonnie's for a night but then Bonnie said she was too sad and stressed to have us there, with the baby coming soon. A little desperate, we decided to go camping.

For the next week we drove between beaches along the central coast, walked, wrote, drank beer and slept in Gene's old car. Michael wrote a list of mad plans for the future, plans that involved him getting paid work somewhere, recording his album, singing at a body of water every day, building the 24/7 radio livestream. He was going to give this list to his family, to prove to them that he had a plan. I hoped that Linda would let him stay so he could find some work in the area and save money. I still couldn't think about what I should do but Rebecca had invited me to come live with her in New York for a while and I imagined once I got there I might be able to think straight and figure out what the hell to do next.

'You two need to move on with your own life now,' Linda had told me before we left. I couldn't understand how his family could abandon him at a time like this. I'd had to remind her that Michael had come home to look after Gene, that we'd been living and working in Chicago. At the same time, I got what she was saying and why she couldn't afford to have him hanging around if it was going to be like it had always been – him staying there to work on his music non-stop and not earning any money. Michael was a liability, too much for this world, and I was an angel apparently so it was up to me to find a place in it for him. But I was no angel and I could barely look after myself. He needed a lawyer or a teacher, someone with a routine and a steady pay cheque and their feet on the ground. Even while we made plans for the future at the beach, my heart wasn't in it. I felt deeply responsible for him and at the same time deeply incapable of giving him what he needed. I needed peace too. I was exhausted. He was never going to give me peace. I could see what it was that scared his family. He could turn on you and take from you in the blink of an eye. He had so much love to give but his love had teeth. Under the surface was always the ticking possibility that his love was about to flip and bite your head off, eat your head up, spit it out and say: 'What's wrong with you? You're all chewed up. Your lights are dimming. You're all chewed up and the lights are off. Poor girl. Poor girl!'

Gene didn't have a funeral. They were going to take his ashes out to the ocean in the spring. After the week of camping, Linda got lonely and wanted Michael back in the house again. I decided it was the right time to leave and Michael agreed he would stay and work and look after his mom. We found him a job doing yard work for a neighbour. He would save some money and in January we would figure out a plan. He wanted to save up and travel around the country. I didn't believe he would ever make it out of there.

As we left for the train station, a commode arrived for Gene, more than a month late.

Linda couldn't bear to look at it, so we said we'd give

it to Goodwill on the way to the station. She gave us a trash bag of old blankets to donate too. I said a tearful goodbye to Linda and she handed me an envelope with a hundred-dollar bill in it. She thanked me for all the help and told me to get something nice for myself.

'Michael doesn't want you to go,' she said. 'But it's a lot here. He really loves you. He's much happier when you're together. But you can have breaks when you don't see each other. That's good for relationships too.'

'Mom,' Michael said, giving her a hug. 'It's time to stop talking now.'

I hugged her too and got in the car.

'I never say goodbye,' she said. 'I only say see you later.'

We drove up to the back of Goodwill and waved down a man who seemed to be accepting donations.

'Is that a commode?' he asked.

'Yep. My dad just died. He never used it.'

He shook his head and tutted. 'Nah. We can't take that. That's nasty.'

'How about these blankets?' Michael said, pointing to the trash bag.

'This bag? Those blankets?' The man took a quick sideways look. 'Nah, we can't take that either. That's nasty too.'

We were in a silly mood, driving to San Luis Obispo with the commode rattling in the back. It was a fresh December day. You could feel a change in the air. We stopped off at Ben Franklin's Deli and I ordered three Californian sandwiches from the cashier, one for me, one for Michael, and one for him to bring home to his mom. The woman who served us was missing a lot of teeth and couldn't understand me.

'My dad just passed away and my girlfriend is leaving for New York!' Michael announced out of nowhere.

We ate our sandwiches at a sunny table at the back of the shop beside a mural of a California mountain scene.

'I don't think she likes us,' I said.

'Yeah, it must be because you have teeth.'

'That's nasty!'

There was still some time before the train. At the station we ran up over the footbridge to get a good view of the tracks and the hills. I took a few pictures of Michael. He took a few of me. The train came, we said goodbye, and I found a spot with a table at the back of the second-floor observation car, the same booth we'd sat in after that first trip.

My bags stowed away, I looked down and saw Michael on the platform below, dancing to get my attention. He was trying to say something, but I couldn't understand him. He mimed and danced around a bit more. Got on his knees. Drew a picture of a house with his finger in the air.

A man sitting a few seats ahead of me watched the scene in awe. All of a sudden he began narrating it to the rest of the car.

'Marry me,' the man said. 'We'll have a house by the sea.'

Michael mimed writing in a notebook, then swimming, then playing guitar.

'You can write poetry. I'll swim. Play music,' said the man.

By this time everyone in the observation car was watching. The narrator turned to me. 'Does he have a phone number? I want to tell him something.'

'He doesn't have a phone,' I said. 'But you can leave a message on his mother's answering machine.'

So the man dialled Linda's number, and Michael, feeding off the audience, mimed a phone in response. I thought of Linda at home alone, rattled by the phone ringing. The man spoke to Michael through the glass and Michael nodded along, though he definitely couldn't hear. Neither of them broke eye contact. The man said he was a preacher. He'd married about a hundred couples by now. Each time it had been uniquely special. 'Why wait?' he told the future Michael, who would be listening to his mother's answering machine if he ever got around to it. The preacher ended his message with his number, saying to call him if we wanted to get married.

The train started moving and Michael ran along the platform. I waved until I could no longer see him. All this talk about marriage in God's country. No doubt the two men had envisioned a wonderful life for us. Like the life Linda now said she and Gene had once had. Rich with love and music. Rich with the sound of Linda singing in the kitchen and crying in the Blue Room. Gene saying: *Thank you, son.* Gene's dead body . . . just wheeled off in the night while the chihuahua watched in Linda's arms, the only time I ever saw it not growling.

Soon I was coasting inland. A rush of green-gold on either side. Pesticide farmland, trees, bushes thick with leaves, sunlight gracing the tip of everything. I stared out the window the whole journey. No sign of December anywhere, no sign of time passing. It seemed just like spring.

Lucy

A sad and cosy Christmas, a sad New Year's Eve. And now a very cold and gloomy January, depressed in Brooklyn, staying with my best friend Rebecca, sharing her lumpy bed in a sad and dusty brownstone she'd recently moved into after having her heart terribly broken. She was a wreck and so was I. It felt like the first winter of my life, after leaving the land of California and Michael and his dad dying, with no plan about what to do next. But the apartment really was dusty and depressing. Dark wood-panelled walls, dirty windows, dirty cream curtains, dusty old books on the shelves above the panels in the dining room. She shared the place with a frosty girl who worked for a hip towel company, and there was a pile of colourful, geometric towels in the dark dining room. It would be so nice to own a beautiful towel, I thought, every time I caught sight of them.

The apartment could have been beautiful too, in its eccentric, historic brownstone way, but it needed a good clean. We needed to give it a good clean. There was a large, totally empty room beside Rebecca's which her friend from film school would be moving in to at the end of the month and we could have made use of too, but we didn't have the energy. Rebecca bought a fresh new duvet cover for her room and I bought some new winter boots for myself, and that was the best we could do. From her bedroom on those early January mornings, we heard the frosty room-mate put on her own heeled boots and head out to work. Rebecca would then bring us the girl's leftover coffee from the pot and get back under the covers. I'd peek out the misty window and look down on the girl clip-clopping through the dark morning, off to go and market towels, and I'd feel at the same time terribly sad and terribly cosy and glad that I had nowhere to go on this strange, cold month outside of life with Rebecca beside me, both of us with our warm coffee and aching hearts, under the new covers, on top of the lumpy bed. I'm sure the girl thought we were very odd.

We were woken up on the morning of the 6th of January by my phone ringing with a number from Northampton, Massachusetts. I only knew one person from that area code and I was not ready to talk to her so early in the morning, but Rebecca nudged me and so I answered. Through the speaker came the very awake and manic and hopefully not drunk voice of my Aunt Lucy. She told me she was calling because it would have been my dad's seventieth birthday today. Had I forgotten? Did I remember when we visited her in Northampton for my dad's fiftieth birthday, twenty years ago? She'd taken us to a fish restaurant where my dad ate two lobsters. Did I realise that was the last time I'd seen her? Didn't I remember? I did! And I remembered the bib he wore that had a drawing of a lobster wearing a bib and eating a lobster. I also remembered that Lucy and my dad had argued the whole time and had both relapsed into drinking by the end of the visit and we did not return as a family again. I didn't say that, though, because Lucy didn't wait for an answer. She was busy telling me how she'd already been up for hours and made two batches of cupcakes before the sun rose. She said she'd heard from my brother that I was in New York for a while. She said I should come visit. She said New England winters were hard, the hardest, but she was doing the best she could. She said she missed my father, especially on his birthday, but she loved the children he'd left behind. Twenty years, twenty winters. That really had been the last time I'd seen her. But she and my father would talk all the time on the phone when I was growing up. Early rambling phone calls before the rest of the world and their families woke up, sharing recipes, getting overexcited about the birds and spring flowers, until either one of them crashed or started an argument or started drinking again and then there would be months of no phone calls. Lucy would still call the house, even after he died – on birthdays and holidays and Christmas and at three in the morning, manic or drunk or just mad and chatty, and it was very difficult to get off the phone. Was she drunk now? It was hard to tell but I thought not. She was saying how she was about to bake another batch of cakes for her colleagues at Lowe's gardening centre and that seemed hopeful.

Rebecca pulled her confused, sleepy head out of the covers and I managed to interrupt Lucy to say that I had to go, the friend I was staying with was sleeping beside me. 'OK, sweetie,' Lucy said. 'But I'm going to call you tomorrow and you're gonna book a train to visit.'

That evening Lucy sent me a series of pictures she'd taken from an old family album. There was one particularly striking picture of her parents, Patty and Frank Senior, slouching against a car in Philadelphia just before they were married and Frank joined the Marines. In the photo he is tall and comically square-shouldered, smug and scowling in his uniform, and my grandmother looks very tiny and beautiful and unhappy beside him. It made you want to tell this grim, handsome couple leaning uncomfortably by a car to stay the hell away from each other.

But Lucy sent other, sweeter pictures too. One of my father and my Uncle Kimber playing soccer. One of Uncle Kimber with his senior prom date. Another of the best-friend-neighbour's-kids turned step-siblings, posing on a lawn in their striped T-shirts and bell-bottoms, looking high, like they were having a lot of fun all together in their crazy blended family. The last one she sent was of Lucy and my dad and their brother

Kimber and their elder sister Helen when they were still children, sitting on a wall: bare feet; silly, sharp, bony grins. I showed the picture to Rebecca. It was just Helen and Lucy left at that point. Uncle Kimber had drunk himself to death a few years before my dad did. I'd heard my Aunt Helen was about to do the same.

'You have to visit,' Rebecca said. 'I think it could be important.'

'But I'm a mess! And Lucy might be drunk or crazy. If I leave you, I might become a mush or a splat.'

'A mush in boots! We'll get you there and back.'

A few days later, I had an early train booked to Springfield, Massachusetts, the closest station to Lucy's house, and Rebecca and I were up earlier than the room-mate, clip-clopping through the dark morning to the subway. We parted at Penn Station and she carried on uptown to her university, far earlier than she needed to, but hey, she was getting me there! It felt very strange to get on a train with my backpack and be by myself. I did feel like a mush in boots. When was the last time I'd spent any hours alone? The flight to New York, the train from Nipomo. And before that? No idea. And now I was on the train to Springfield. Springfield, as in *The Simpsons*. Pandora and I had hardly been able to believe we were going to be going through *Simpsons* Springfield on the way to Lucy's on that last millennium visit twenty years ago, even after our parents tried to explain that there were hundreds of Springfields in America. Springfield was an Everytown. Like the Sims. Like Pleasant Hill, California, where Rebecca was from. Like Nipomo where Michael was currently working as a farmhand to a nice old couple, building a fence and looking after horses and saving to come this way. I missed him and his golden Everytown, here on the Northeast Regional line passing boarded-up houses and piles of dirty snow. It didn't make sense for him to come east but I couldn't go back there either. A plan! I needed Rebecca to tell me what to do. Every time I tried to think of a plan or a life further ahead than the next day, a sliding door of darkness came down and all was dark and day-less. A paralysing plan-less day-less life of dirty snow, no time, no days, no home, no idea what to do or have for dinner. Rebecca had told me to come to New York and so I'd come to New York. She'd told me to go see Lucy and so I was on my way to see Lucy. At least today I was on the rails with a full day ahead of me and a person to see who was part of my family, even if she was nuts and I hadn't seen her in so long.

Lucy was waiting on the platform to greet me, holding a fake red rose. Big blue eyes, thin face, wispy blonde hair cut close to her head. 'It's been twenty years! I just had to meet you with a rose.'

She took my arm and marched me to the car. Thirty minutes later we were at her house. A small blue wooden house on a suburban street that seemed to be the shape of a hexagon or a heptagon or a square-edged star. Lucy jumped out of the car and rushed me too, saying, 'Come on, slowpoke, we have less than forty-eight hours and there's lots to do!'

Her third husband stood in the doorway. All I knew about this man was that she'd met him five years before at an AA meeting and married him without telling any of her children. He greeted me with a frail handshake and smiled somewhat vacantly but I don't remember much else. Not if he was in the house for the rest of the visit or if he went somewhere else or if he was just sitting in the corner the whole time, as a chair or a ghost might sit in the corner the whole time without anyone noticing. He shook my hand in the sunny doorway, somewhat hunched and unwell, vacant but kindly. Then my aunt pulled me inside and her husband dissolved into dust.

Lucy was manic today. That was the first thing she said when we got through the door, apologising for being so hyper. 'It's a problem we all have. Had. My brothers, my sister and me.' She took me to almost every corner of her strangely shaped house, showing me photos, magnets, pots in the cupboard, cookbooks, novelty mugs, clothes on a rail, a T-shirt – her favourite T-shirt – from a jazz festival she'd gone to years ago, that she said her brother, my father, would have loved. She took the T-shirt off the hanger and gave it to me. I objected: 'But it's your favourite T-shirt!' She ran down the stairs – 'Wear it for the day then!' – leaving me to change, and, when I got back downstairs, she'd prepared us tea and cookies. She'd made the cookies this morning and cooked extra to give other people throughout the day. 'Helen, here's something you should know about your Aunt Lucy. I bake the best cookies. It makes me very popular.' She put five on my plate. I was still eating the first cookie when she had her hat and coat on and we and the cookies were out the door. I'd already forgotten I was depressed, forgotten I was a person, or a mess or a splat. Perhaps I was becoming dust too. Maybe that was just what happened to anyone caught in the sixty-mile-an-hour whirlwind monologue of a day in a life with Lucy.

First stop was just down the road to a neighbour's house. She wanted to show me a quilt they'd been making together for her son's wedding. She held the quilt over her head – a vertical landscape of red to blue to green to red – and decided she should work on it while we were here. I sat on a chair in the corner of the room by a pile of fabric. Lucy would ask me a question. How was my mother? Why did she never answer the phone? Had she offended her in some way? Could my mother still vote in the US? Had I requested my ballot yet? Did I know that she, Lucy, had once run for mayor and had two law degrees? And when I was in the middle of answering one question, she'd ask me another or just start talking about something else. She told me the impressive achievements of her crazy-smart children. One had started a carbon-capture non-profit. Another was doing a PhD on the war in Iraq. She was incredibly proud. Of course she'd taught them everything they knew. She'd given them brains, that's for sure. Each of her five children knew how to read before they'd even started school. And now her son was getting married and she wouldn't be going to the ceremony, it was too far away and she couldn't pay for the flight, but she was making the quilt instead, this was what she could do. She turned to her neighbour friend. 'You know this is the first time I've seen my niece in twenty years! Can you believe it? And can you believe how awesome this quilt is?' She held the quilt up proudly over her head again.

'It's very beautiful,' I said, and felt a burst of sorrow for Lucy and the quilt in front of her face and her son who had a loving quilt for his wedding instead of a mother.

'I would do anything for my kids,' Lucy said. 'And they're the ones I've hurt the most.'

And loved the most too, I might have said but probably didn't because I was a mute mote of dust and the day was young and soon we were off again. Next, she drove us to the Smith Botanic Garden. She ordered me to pretend to kiss a cactus and took photos. She got someone to take another photo of the two of us in a part of the garden that looked like a jungle, with the plan to put the picture online with a caption about us being on a trip in Mexico. Back to her house for salami sandwiches. She sat me down on the sofa of her living room and she performed entire songs from her rock choir. Soon I was joining in too, still sitting, while she danced around the room to Queen in a pink bandana, reminding me of Edie from *Grey Gardens*, a film I'd just watched with Rebecca during our sad and cosy Christmas for two.

Back up the stairs to show me all the family photos. Back out the door: we were going to the other side of town, where she had invited herself to a friend's mother's house to join the end of their family lunch party. I sat with the very lovely family in their living room while they finished their lunch and asked me about England and the Queen and what I thought about America. The whole time Lucy ran around outside playing ball with the seven-year-old boy. Every so often, I saw her pink bandana sprinting past a window. After an hour or so, we left the lovely family and went back to Lucy's so that she could get dinner ready. Her youngest daughter, Netta, came over with her boyfriend and we chatted while Lucy cooked up a pork stew, one of my dad's old recipes. Netta asked me if her mother was driving me mad and I told her that it felt just like home, which was true. The stew was delicious, it tasted like ten years ago, when my dad was alive. Afterwards we all played a card game that seemed to basically be an excuse for Lucy and Netta and Netta's boyfriend to slap each other on the hands. I was dreaming of a cold bottle of beer. And then it was midnight. Netta and her boyfriend left. Lucy put some popcorn in the oven for a midnight snack and began to tell me about the death of her brother Kimber.

'When I found out that Kimber was in hospital with

liver failure – that he was dying – I called your dad, told him our brother was dying and told him not to come. I knew it would be a disaster. But he was a stubborn bastard so of course he came.'

Lucy then told me that when their sister Helen arrived at the hospital she was drunk and when my dad arrived at the hospital, flying all the way from England, he was drunk too. They had a huge argument because Lucy wouldn't give my dad Kimber's car keys. He told her: 'If you don't give me those keys you will have another dead brother on your hands.' Eventually they put him in a taxi and he went back to Uncle Kimber's place. Lucy was the only sober one at this point, or so the story went tonight, while we waited for the corn to pop. She told me she arranged for the hospital staff to turn off Uncle Kimber's machine without consulting her drunk siblings. And the next day, her brother Kimber dead, she arrived at his house in the suburbs of Washington DC to find my dad fully dressed and passed out drunk in their dead brother's bed. There were a few empty bottles of vodka on the floor beside him. She said my dad had finished off the same bottle that had killed their brother.

'It's just the kind of twisted thing he would do,' she told me. She said she'd sat on the edge of Kimber's bed and cried. She told my dad: 'I need my big brother!' and then she just left him there and they didn't speak to each other for a year. As she told me this, her eyes filled with tears. I could remember them not speaking for a long time after Uncle Kimber died but Dad's story was different. He was so angry that she'd let the doctors turn off the machine that was keeping Kimber alive without consulting him.

'You'd think after that I'd come home and never drink again. Of course that's the first thing I did.' She wiped her tears, brought the popcorn out of the microwave and in minutes she was on her knees, for a dramatic reading from a book of William Blake's poems that my dad had sent her when he was in college. First, 'London', which she said was his favourite: *I wander thro' each charter'd street, / Near where the charter'd Thames does flow. / And mark in every face I meet / Marks of weakness, marks of woe.* And ending with 'A Poison Tree', which she said was her favourite: *I was angry with my foe: / I told it not, my wrath did grow.*

'If you feed poisonous feelings they get you in the end,' Lucy said. 'Just look at my family.'

I was no longer dust. I was a person again and I was exhausted and had a pounding headache. I told Lucy I had to go to sleep, which might have been the first thing I'd said for hours. She gave me her bed and slept or didn't sleep in the living room – I could hear her moving below. I put my head on her pillow, thinking of Michael and addiction and brothers and sisters and mothers and fathers and all the things she'd told me. When I opened my eyes again it was morning and I was a child and my dad was waking me up for school but he was a woman now and I was twenty-eight years old, with a terrible headache, waking up in my Aunt Lucy's bed after not seeing her for twenty years. 'It's time to wake up, sleepyhead!' Lucy had come into the room and was opening the curtains. Such a bright morning. It didn't feel like I'd slept at all. The house smelled like coffee and toast and brownies. Outside, the months of snow had melted overnight. 'This shouldn't be happening in January, but it's a beautiful day!' There was a big spread on the kitchen table and I ate it all, trying to keep my eyes open while Lucy cleaned up and opened things and closed things and toasted things and banged the whole world around, is how it felt, while the sun slanted into her funny hexagonal house from every angle, in dusty strobes of pale light. Triangles and hexagons and octagons of light. And was her husband there? Sitting at the table or in a chair by a window or helping her clean up too? Was he a ghost to begin with? And was I there? Did I dream it? Did the leaves fall? Did the snow melt? Was it really the morning? Weren't the winters hard? Wasn't it still winter? Didn't my head ache? Wasn't it time to go?

We got in the car and she drove me back to the train station. Across the pretty sidewalks of Northampton, all the moms and the dads and the kids and the tricycles were out. The lawns were squashed and grey-gold from months of snow. Lucy seemed worn, perhaps because for the first time she wasn't speaking. She held the steering wheel tight, with bony calloused hands, a gardener's hands, a depressive gardener who loved the spring. Was Lucy crashing? Was she thinking of drink? Wasn't it a lovely morning for January?

'It wasn't our parents' fault. It's in our genes,' she said, breaking the silence. 'They didn't show us the love we needed, but they didn't know how. They were young and traumatised and stunted.'

I told her I was thinking of visiting Granny soon too. She was ninety-seven and lived in the same depressing retirement home in Philadelphia we had visited all those years ago.

Lucy said, don't bother. 'She's a cold-hearted woman. You know it took me a year to bury Kimber. My father was dead by then too and my mother just refused.'

I told her I didn't know anything about it and she quickly told me how she'd had Kimber's ashes in a FedEx box in her kitchen. On the year anniversary of his death she organised a burial, drove to my granny's retirement home outside of Philadelphia and made her get in the car. They drove up to the Quaker graveyard and Granny wouldn't get out of the car. She didn't explain why, didn't say anything, just stared ahead and ignored her daughter when she begged her to get out of the car.

'My mother can't acknowledge anything depressing,' she said. 'When I took a train down to Philadelphia to tell her that your father had died, all she said was: "Why?" I said to her: "Why are you asking why?

Why don't you just cry!" And my mother said: "I don't cry." That was the end of the conversation.'

Out the window the gold grass shone. I was seeing all the identical bungalows, the driveways and the cars like my first trip to Massachusetts. Springfield like *The Simpsons*, like the Sims, like every town's Everytown. Somewhere . . . fields of spring, if we could just get through this winter.

'I don't have many good things to say about my mother. I haven't seen her in years. I just can't take it. But I'm not trying to hold a grudge. I'm trying to just get on with my life . . . AA every morning. I'm making a quilt. You've seen it! I cook. I bake. I volunteer. I have supportive friends. Three psychiatrists. Another degree. A course on sustainability. A job looking after plants at Lowe's. Pills to sleep. Coffee in the morning. Lost two brothers to drink, about to lose a sister. My children come and visit but I know it's a chore. I can tell. I get it . . . I've put them through hell . . . And still . . . I'm only ever three minutes away from going to the store and getting a drink.' She paused for a moment. 'Helen, listen. Even after everything . . . after all that I've gone through, after losing half my family to drink, after everything I do to try not to drink, and all the pain I've caused my children – if I could just find a way to drink and do it safely. If I could just find a room and be left there just to drink . . . I would still do it.'

She turned on to the highway.

'I'm not meant to be in this world,' she said. 'I don't

fit. I'm too much. It's too hard. Drinking is the only thing that makes me feel normal.'

We got to the station and I had only a few minutes to make my train. There was so much I wanted to say to her and I was trying to hold on to and remember everything she'd told me. The tragedy of what happened to each of those siblings . . . I would never be able to understand it.

'I know it's hard,' I told her then, something like that. 'But I can see how much you are trying.'

'Today is a good day,' she said. Her eyes were big and sad. It shocked me all over again just how much she looked like my dad. 'I take it day by day.'

I hugged her. 'We won't leave it twenty years!'

I got back on the train, holding my rose so that it wouldn't be crushed in my bag. Twenty years, twenty winters. Did I know that this would be the last time I'd ever see her? That she'd die a few years later, the same way as her brothers, and on the first day of spring? I think I must have.

As the train left I called Rebecca. She said she would meet me at Penn Station and take us home. She had a craving for chilli dogs. And she had news too. The frosty girl was moving out and I could move in officially at the end of the month. I didn't know how I could pay for it and also . . . what about Michael?

'Something to think about,' Rebecca said. 'Wouldn't it be good to stay in one place for a while? And if Michael made it here too then that would be something.'

I wanted so badly to hang a nice towel on the back of a door and unpack a bag into a chest of drawers and I knew that if I told Michael to, he would come running, even if it made zero sense for us to suddenly move into an apartment in such an expensive and difficult city. I couldn't imagine the future so didn't need to worry about it. Day by day. I was taking it day by day too.

That night, Rebecca and I took a broom to the empty room beside hers and made up a song about brooms and dust and rooms. I tied the red rose to the door handle. It was my first belonging in New York City.

I didn't hear anything more from Lucy and had a feeling she had gone straight home to drink. There was something about the look on her face. It was the same defeated look my father had, the last time I saw him.

He'd driven me to the airport; I was moving to California for university and he was going back to an empty house. I just knew that would be the last time I saw him. And wasn't I right? Didn't Lucy basically tell me this? But wasn't life hard? And didn't they try? Wasn't I loved? Couldn't I have visited her again? Didn't they do the best that they could?

If I didn't have Rebecca's chilli-dog meal and lumpy bed and if I was an alcoholic too . . . I don't know why I wouldn't have found a warm, safe room to lock myself inside and do exactly the same.

Lost Boys

Linda didn't want to look at her dead husband's van in the drive any more. It had been almost two years since Gene had died, and Michael and I were still sharing a room in Brooklyn after breaking up half-heartedly and getting straight back together several times.

She sent us the book *Men Are from Mars, Women Are from Venus*, along with a loving note saying she was going to give the van away if he didn't come back to get it soon. We had miraculously saved up some money from pandemic unemployment checks and Michael convinced me to rent out our room and come back to California with him to rescue the vehicle – the only thing left to him from his father. 'We need to be moving,' he said. 'A new context changes everything. It's so obviously the right choice for us.'

We stayed in Nipomo for a week. He took out the back seats, built a wooden platform inside that would fit a single mattress on top and a bunch of his dad's old musical equipment below. The 2002 Toyota Sienna would not break down in the middle of America, he assured me: it had the spirit of Gene on its side now. We found a tin of paint in the garage and painted the mattress platform Big Country Blue.

In other cars, Michael drove like a maniac but I felt safe beside him in the Sienna. Leaving Nipomo, we played an Allman Brothers CD of his dad's that we found in the glovebox. The old car hummed along, going never more than sixty miles an hour, and it seemed, with the sun and the wind and green rushing past the open windows, that we were living again the life we were supposed to be living – on the move and together. The plan was to camp around and then make our way up to Santa Cruz in time for our friend Cameron's thirtieth birthday. From there we would slowly drive back east and catch up with the rest of our problems then.

Cachuma, Jalama, Pismo. Chumash names for beaches and lakes filled with RVs in the weekdays. When we camped on a grassy cliff at Manresa Beach, Michael caught a cold and so I spent some days alone, while he slept in the tent. One afternoon I just followed a black beetle all around on the beach. Where was it going? One two, one two. Up the dunes, down the dunes. Following the beetle – with Michael safe up on the cliff, but not beside me – I felt totally at peace. I had no thoughts or desires, except to follow the beetle. Until the evening came and I wanted to hold on to the feeling, to cup it in my hands and keep it for ever. But how could I? The beetle marched on into the sunset and the next morning we drove up to Santa Cruz.

A high-noon sun hung over so many people out on a Saturday. Parking on a side street near Seabright Beach I spotted Pero down the block, emerging from a beat-up Toyota of his own. I hadn't seen him in maybe three years. Michael called out to him and he came running.

'You got skinny and I got fat!' Pero said when we hugged. He did have more of a chin and a little round belly. He combed a hand through his short, greasy hair. Tiny flecks of scalp landed on his black T-shirt. '*Pero*, I am not doing good,' he said, in the little voice he used with his best friends.

We followed Pero back to his car and he told us that his grandad had died, three weeks ago. It had just been the funeral. He'd driven up from Costa Mesa that morning in the car his grandad had left to him before he died. He pulled out a case of beer from the front seat and pocketed a quart of whiskey from a backpack on the floor. There were crushed beer cans strewn about the car already and a bobble head of the Pope attached to the dashboard, with his hands raised up to the sky. '*Pero*, I am not good,' he said again as he slammed the door.

Pero was really a boy called Matt from Orange County, California. People called him Pero in college because he started a lot of sentences with *pero*, the Spanish word for 'but', and also because he was very much like a *perro*. Loyal, excitable, a needy pain. Quick to anger, quick to wrestle, quick to run up into the mountains in a rage and sleep in the woods. He had the darting blue eyes of a dog, which were really the darting eyes of a boy fed Adderall from the age of seven to encourage him to behave, sit still and be a good *perro*.

He talked at us non-stop as we headed to the beach to find the party. It had been a bad few years. The pandemic had been brutally lonely for him. He said that the night his grandad died he'd been alone in San Francisco. He got fucked up, fell off his electric scooter, messed up his back and now couldn't do his shifts at the hospital. 'I work in the ER now,' he said. 'Did you know that? I've got a real big-daddy job.' The job required a lot of heavy lifting and he couldn't do that with a spent back. So he'd been off for two weeks, drinking whiskey and missing his grandpa. He really missed his grandpa. A good man, humble and kind. More like a dad to him than his own dad, long lost to drink and TV.

Cameron, his girlfriend Teddy and a few others were playing volleyball at the far end of the beach, with face masks under their chins. Jack was lying slightly apart from the group. He had his head resting on a backpack, long legs crossed with shoes on. He slowly rose when he saw us approaching and came in for a bony hug.

'What's wrong with you, Jack?' I asked.

'Nothing's wrong,' he said and made an attempt to smile.

In the time I hadn't seen him, Jack had turned twenty-eight, then twenty-nine, been sworn into a woke fraternity in Berkeley (where he was not a student) through some pandemic loophole, forgone his playwriting dreams to be paid a lot of money working in Facebook's augmented reality department, and lost a front tooth playing basketball. The week after his tooth was knocked out he'd lost his dad to a heart attack too. When he told me the news in October over the phone he'd said: 'If your dad died and he was an asshole does it count as much?' Then he'd called back on video to show me the gaping hole in his mouth. He had big teeth. The missing one left quite the hole.

We sat down next to him and made our way through the beer until the beer ran out and Pero threw a fit. 'No one ever brings enough beer!' He gathered some cash from Cameron, the most generous and well-adjusted boy of the bunch, and charged off to go get some more. Soon, he was back beside me, passed out with his head resting on a plate of melon rinds.

Jack woke Pero up by pouring a bottle of water over his head. Pero shot up and launched himself at Michael. The three got wrestling. He used to be able to pin down the both of them with one hand each but now they tackled him to the ground. Michael on his head and Jack on his legs.

'You're fat, Pero! What happened to you?'

His voice came from under Michael: 'My grandpa died!'

It was not the reunion I had imagined but when are they ever? More people played volleyball. Others jumped in the freezing ocean. I chatted with someone's girlfriend who didn't like ball games either. Something had gone missing in the weirdness of the last few years but I couldn't place exactly what that was. What makes a day memorable? At some point it was just me and moody Jack sitting on the sand. I asked him what was wrong. His job? His dad? His life? Why was he all twisted up? He shook his head and sucked his cheeks. He said he just had code brain from an intense week of work and it was irritating – my constant emotional monitoring.

'Well, I'm sorry but I haven't seen you in years and your mood stinks.'

For a moment he smiled and the light came back. He said I was probably right about his life and his job but he wasn't grieving his dad. 'It's scary,' he said. 'It's what a waste of life feels like. When you look back and there's nothing to latch on to, just wisps of memories, things that could have happened that didn't become anything.'

I stared at the plate of melon rinds Pero had passed out on. Where had he gone?

Pero called as the sun was setting. Michael and I were at a gas station on the way out of Santa Cruz. He screamed down the phone: 'You fucking bitch! You took my dongle!' I could hear a road raging under tyres in the background. I told him I didn't know what a dongle was and also that was no way to talk to a person. Then I hung up.

'He's a psychopath!' I said. 'Raging about a dongle. What's a dongle?' Michael cracked up and pointed to the thing that was attached to the aux cord.

Maybe I should have called him back and said, 'Pero, you're drunk out of your mind, you should not be driving right now. And yes, I do have your dongle. I didn't mean to take it!' But I did not. And not long after that phone call, Pero was stopped for speeding and arrested for being one hundred per cent over the legal limit in his dead grandad's car.

Jack had invited Michael and me to stay at his Berkeley fraternity for the weekend. When we arrived he snuck us in through the back. It turned out, as we should have expected, that we weren't really welcome and he was kind of outstaying his welcome too.
 'Because you're too old? Why didn't you tell us!'
 'We can just stay in my room. It will be fine.'
 So we hid in Jack's room for the night, and did not explore the grand historic mansion. His twenty-two-year-old girlfriend Issy came by and over Modelo and pizza she impressed Michael and Jack with knowledge from a class she was taking on swarm theory, AI and aliens. The two boys nodded and ogled and chipped in now and again.
 'We're a domesticated species.'
 'We already know they live among us.'
 She mentioned something about silver fox experiments. What was that? She told us all about scientists in Russia who domesticated foxes in the thirties or forties by breeding the tamest foxes with the tamest foxes until they were sweet-natured and friendly to humans. And by

doing that discovering there was a gene associated with tameness that gave animals across the board floppy ears and cute faces. I asked her what that had to do with aliens. From the other side of the room, Michael raised his big eyebrows at me and made a face that meant – I told you so, I told you so. They live among us. I told you so.

No one had a real answer for me. We're a sick, domesticated species. Foxes can be bred floppy-eared and afraid of the wild. Maybe we did that to ourselves or maybe it was the aliens. I was feeling bored and ignored. I got into Jack's bed and fell asleep.

In the morning, Jack took back his invitation and said we better go stay with Pero instead. He cooked up scrambled eggs on toast and we waited for the eggs on the stoop outside the mansion because we weren't allowed in the kitchen either. Michael danced and ran up and down the grand stone steps. He was wearing one sandal and one shoe.

'Why are you doing that?'

'Because we're in Berkeley. And in Berkeley you can run up and down the stairs like a dog and you can wear one sandal and one shoe.'

Pero lived in the Presidio, near Crissy Field Beach. He'd wangled a studio apartment in an old military barracks through a deal which had something to do with his catering side-job.

We spent the day in Berkeley and drove over there in the early evening. When we arrived he'd just got off the phone to a lawyer and seemed to be very drunk already. It was going to be a big charge, he said. Maybe ten thousand. Maybe a criminal record. God. He popped a tall can of IPA.

His apartment depressed the hell out of me. The dark blinds were pulled down behind his electric drum kit, but licks of golden hour came in through the sides. He had a hotpot hob and a mini fridge. There was a tapestry of a mountain scene hung behind his bed and another of a pine forest by the drum set. On the other side of the room above a grey Ikea sofa bed was a canvas of a wolf licking its lips. The floor was littered with dirty clothes and plates and sandwich wrappers and crushed cans. Between the toilet and the basin in the bathroom was a tall blue bin filled to the top with more cans and all kinds of mini liquor bottles swimming amongst the tin.

Pero paced around his studio apartment, talking on a loop. Ten thousand dollars, a criminal record. Ten thousand dollars, a criminal record. I couldn't sit still listening to him so I opened a beer and started cleaning up the place. Threw some more cans and bottles in the overflowing bin. Collected dirty plates and put his laundry in a basket.

'Do you just cook all your meals on this?' I asked, pointing at the hotpot hob. Pero said there was a communal kitchen on the first floor of the building but he mainly lived off deli sandwiches and food from his catering gigs, then he went back to his ranting.

'OK, Pero,' Michael said. 'I'm setting the timer for thirty minutes. Every time you mention your DUI during this thirty minutes I will drink one of your beers.'

'Michael!' Pero yelled. 'I'm gunna have to pay ten thousand dollars, this is my reality.'

'That's one time so far.' He got up and pulled a beer out of the mini fridge. Pero cackled his throaty little laugh. Then he launched himself at Michael and tried to wrestle the beer out of his hands. Michael took a wide stance and held the beer above his head.

'Everything is constructed, Pero,' Michael said, still holding the beer above his head. 'You have ultimate control over how you view the world.'

'Shut the fuck up, Michael!' Pero said.

'Yep, the truth hurts. Most people can't handle it.'

Pero got hold of Michael's wrist and pulled it down with his whole body. They both fell and knocked into the corner of the room, screaming and kicking and cackling.

What was I doing here? Back with Michael again and cleaning up drunk messes. I couldn't remember making any decisions. Seemed like I must have never made a decision in my life. Pieces of me were falling off in the room amongst the plates and cans and laundry and I was trying to clean up and collect those too.

I got out of there quickly and headed for the communal kitchen with a pile of dirty dishes. On my way I heard Michael's steps behind me and the hiss of a can of beer. He handed me the one he'd hidden in his pocket.

'I didn't forget about you, Melon.'

We drank our beers in a sunny spot by the car and brought in our own dirty camping dishes, along with some tins of chopped tomato to make pasta sauce.

By the time we'd finished cooking, eating and cleaning up, the windows in the communal kitchen were dark. We brought up a bowl of pasta for Pero. He was passed out on top of his bed with his shoes still on.

Very early the next morning, I woke up on the sofa to Pero opening the front door. He had his jacket done up over his chin.

'Where are you going?'

'Eggs.'

'Eggs?' I asked. He walked out the door.

'Let's get out of here while he's gone,' Michael said.

The beach was empty. The morning light, pale and misty. A heavy wind blowing from the blue hills of Marin. The Golden Gate Bridge, red, red gates of heaven or hell, appearing and disappearing in the fog.

We found a sheltered spot by a grassy dune, a beautiful fenced-in dune of pink and purple wildflowers. What most of San Francisco once was, according to the sign by the fence. We lay down. I put my head in the crook of Michael's shoulder. The wind and sun rocked me back to sleep. Nothing we needed here; warm, still sand.

Michael calm. I was thinking, or the breeze must have been saying, this was the best of us, the best of us . . .

When we woke up there were hundreds of dogs at the dock of the bay. Ten a.m. on a Monday, this sheltered spot turned into the entrance to doggy junction. Leagues of California's best-paid dog walkers ferried past us with six or seven leads and names to keep them company for the morning.

'Good job, Maggie!'

'Way to go, Pedro!'

'I'm talking to you, Dudley!'

A woman with seven or eight poodles attached to her belt hurried past us saying, 'Come on, honeys! Now, we're going to be good today. Aren't we? No barking!'

The walkers released their leads at the ocean and the dogs ran amok, making friends with other dogs. The poodle lady let the leads pull her along so she became one staggering octopus with eight curly, fluffy feet, just jumping for joy. And it made me see it. A dog is not meant to be alone. A dog is man's best friend. We bred them that way. Pero had lived alone in the old military barracks for two years.

In our absence Jack had arrived at the apartment and Pero was back to pacing. 'Where have you been?' Pero asked us and carried on. 'Ten thousand dollars, a criminal record. Ten thousand dollars, a criminal record . . .'

'I kinda shouldn't be here,' Jack whispered to me. He still had his puffer jacket on and his narrow eyes were slinking back and forth between our shoes and the door. 'I have a lot of work to do.'

'Do you actually?'

He laughed and stuck his tongue through the gap in his front teeth.

'Don't leave already,' I pleaded. 'Please don't leave me with them.'

A fresh pack of Tecate sat on the toaster oven with a few cans missing. Michael opened one and Pero screamed at him: 'Get your own beers!'

I felt a strange and familiar discomfort slide down the back of me. I felt every can and bottle in Pero's grim room slide down the back of me. The shame and disorder of someone who cannot stop drinking. What it was like to come home as a child and know that my dad had locked himself in his room with the curtains closed to drink all through the day. Cracks of sun were sliding in through the gaps around the dark blinds here too, and down my back and under my skin, and what was supposed to be out was trying to get in.

'It's probably gunna be a ten-thousand-dollar fine and a criminal record. Apparently you're supposed to consult with a couple of lawyers. So I've spoken to a few now but I can't remember who said what.'

When Pero turned his back I took a beer too.

'Why are you making that face?' Jack said.

'What face?' I said.

'All right!' Jack clapped his hands. He took Pero's hands in his and held them still. 'I'm here to help.'

It was decided that the answer to salvaging the day and saving Pero was recording a song. A pop song. A song about Pero. This was going to be the money maker. Michael pulled out all the music equipment from under the platform in the van and spent an hour setting up to record it. He told Pero that music was the ultimate healer; it elevated everything. 'God and music, Pero. That's what you need.'

I borrowed Pero's scooter and rode to the deli to pick up a sandwich and some more beers. For twenty minutes I was free, scooting along in the sun. I came back to the three of them chanting: 'There's some bones in this house . . . there's some bones in this house . . .' Pero on drums, Jack on guitar. Michael on keys and microphone.

I don't know much about percussion but whatever Pero was doing at the drum set was not even close to keeping a beat. I sat down on the sofa with my sandwich. This apartment was so grim. The wolf licking its lips. They kept chanting along to the sloppy drumming, but their hearts weren't in it. Michael unemployed, unacknowledged Baby Jesus of music. Jack software developer living in a frat with a bunch of twenty-year-olds, missing a front tooth. Pero alcoholic ER technician with a DUI and a messed-up back.

'There's some bones in this house . . . there's some bones in this house . . .' the boys chanted. I could hear the bones of all the drunks and dead fathers we had between us now. First mine, then Michael's, then Jack's.

Pero's father was a wasted alcoholic, but still alive. Michael's dad had not been an alcoholic but for a brief time his mother had been, and so had her own father.

That was as far as they got with the song. After a couple more rounds, Jack put down the guitar and picked up his giant biography of LBJ. Michael rolled a spliff and lit it out the window. Pero downed another beer.

'I knew you would only get a six-pack of light beers, Helen.'

'It's one p.m.'

'Light beers for the morning, IPAs for the afternoon! That's the alchy way!' He laughed and tripped over a cable, spilled beer on a guitar.

'God damn it, Michael!' he cried out.

'That was you, Pero. You're a mess.'

'Why are you wearing one sandal and one shoe?' Pero said. 'Just put on a shoe. You can't just go around doing whatever you want all the time. You make people uncomfortable. And you look crazy. I'm trying not to get kicked off of this place.'

'Pero, you're a raging alcoholic. You pass out in your shoes most nights and you don't even remember it. If you're getting kicked out, that's the reason.'

'Be careful, Michael . . . I'll fight you.'

The walls were closing in. The ceiling was falling down. The habits of youth were not working any more, and of course that was what had happened to our mothers and fathers and their mothers and fathers. When did a life go all wrong? Not overnight but one action led to another, led to another, led to Pero being a full-on drunk now with us here to witness, hopeless and stupid and drunk now ourselves. Where was the beetle of peace? One two, one two, I had drowned the beetle in light beer and now I was dispersed again with no skin and no shape and no way out. The skeletons were falling out of the closets. The bones were rising from the earth. I lay my head down and let it all come.

'Let's take Helen back to the beach,' Michael said.

We found a new spot further west. The dogs had gone. Maybe mushrooms was the answer. Maybe that was what Pero needed or what we all needed. Maybe that was how we could have a nice day and wean him off the drink. Revive his brain or make some new pathways. Maybe it was too late for new pathways. Our destiny was set in stone. Maybe he was too drunk today already anyway. He probably wouldn't feel it. Maybe it was worth a try.

The mushrooms hit me when I was peeing in another fenced-in grassy dune. The grass and the purple flowers swayed in the breeze. I crouched in the grass for a long time. The grains of sand reflected so many tiny suns. My skin was made of sand and grass too. The breeze rippled in my sand and in my hair. I felt very beautiful made of the earth with my trousers down. The thought made me laugh. I was very glad to be away from those monsters in my fenced-in paradise. After a while, though, I missed them.

The three boys were sat in a row with their backs against a brown picket fence, facing the ocean. The wind was much more intense down here by the water but there was something nice about being battered alive. Michael played the guitar and he and Jack made up a new song about Pero.

'My dog got a DUI but he's still my dog . . .' I sat on the guitar case as an audience to watch them. One sandal, one shoe, one toothless, one drunk. Michael does not turn on and off. A dog does not fit in a box. Jack's mind, *the best minds of my generation*, eaten by big tech. So many times in college, just like this, watching these people find some harmony to the dysfunction with their musical instruments. When Michael went missing and committed himself to a mental hospital after almost throwing himself off a bridge on his twenty-first birthday, we got drunk in a cave and Jack got everyone to record a song for him. They didn't know how to talk to each other in any other way. And I suppose I was included in that too because my dad had died in the middle of the year and I wasn't talking about it then either. I was happy to sing in a cave and forget all about it.

I pulled a cold beer from my backpack and watched Michael's hands crawl and pick around his dad's old guitar. Crazy person, but he had a song in his heart that was vital and true. And the song got all twisted up in ugliness and pain and he handed the ugliness on a plate to me daily. 'You're just a lost sad girl who doesn't know what she wants!' he had told me a few days before. He wasn't totally wrong but to be told that constantly only made me more scattered and want to get away from him so I could think straight. But no, I thought, it wasn't just that. Pools of joy and flecks of gold! Pools of joy in his big brown eyes. Life was just more beautiful when he was around. I needed to keep him close and keep him safe and if he was safe I would be safe too. My problem wasn't drinking. What I could not seem to give up was Michael.

'My dog got a DUI but he's still my dog,' the two boys' voices rang out in harmony together.

'I really miss him,' Pero sobbed. 'I miss my grandpa. I'm so sad. I miss him so much.'

Jack's eyes were dark pits and so was the gap where his tooth had been. Michael carried on playing the guitar.

'Write about it, record it. Sing about it,' Jack sang and the wind really picked up. 'Always better than what it was really like at the time.'

'It's OK, Pero,' I said. I rubbed his back and stroked his head and he shuffled his body down and rested his head in the sand. He closed his eyes and fell asleep. The sand of time and a thousand tiny suns was blowing at his face too and filling the crevices of his coat and hat, sticking to his hair and beanie. I was sure if I looked at my hands they would be purple and ancient. I didn't, couldn't look at them. The sand went into his ears, eyes, nose. It was amazing, how quickly he could be buried just by not moving.

'He's sinking,' I said. I wanted to leave him there.

Save him the pain of so much more living, going around and around from father to son to holy ghost to son again.

We pulled Pero up off the ground and sand just poured off him, though a lot of it still remained in his eyes and ears and in the folds of his beanie. He stumbled ahead, crying with his head hung down.

'Why is he dressed like that?' Jack said. 'He looks like a criminal. Like a burglar from *Home Alone*.'

There was something so straightforward about his pain, I thought as he stumbled off. He missed his grandpa, more like a dad to him than his own dad. He was a dog in a man's body. He turned to drink when things got too much and then he could not stop. He did not have a cryptic twist in his brain like the other two.

'Maybe you should go with him,' I said. They ran to catch up with him and took a hand each to walk him home. I fell behind and watched them go. Walking down the road, across the little bridge. Three innocent boys holding hands. I pulled out Michael's little camcorder from my bag and filmed them going. I zoomed in on the back of their heads and panned to their hands, zooming out again. Even Michael – he was just the back of a head holding hands with his two best friends.

I caught up with them at the door to Pero's building.

'Thank you, Helen and Michael,' he said. 'But where were you, Jack? You did nothing!'

'I was holding your hand, Pero!' Jack said.

'No. That was Helen and Michael!'

'No, Pero, it was me.'

We got inside again and Michael and Pero raced for what was left of the beers. Jack slumped on the sofa and scrolled on his phone.

'What's wrong, Jack?' Michael said. 'Working for Facebook is frying your brain!'

Jack looked up from his phone. 'Why are you drinking with him?'

'Wow, Jack. Sounds like you could really use a drink.'

Pero laughed and laughed and tore off his T-shirt. Jack slowly gathered his things, put his backpack on and gave me a hug with no air left in it.

'I'm gunna go look into rehabs,' he said under his breath as he left.

The next morning I woke up, stared at the wolf licking its lips. Beside me on the sofa, Michael's eyes were open too. Cool, brown, staring at the ceiling.

'We can't drink with him today,' I said.

He took some time to respond. 'We'll take him on a sober walk. It will be great. We'll just take him out and keep him walking and then we'll get out of here.'

From across the room, Pero woke up groaning. He got up, shoes still on, and headed straight for the door.

'Where are you going?'

'Eggs.'

'You got eggs yesterday.'

'I just need to get something from my car.'

'What's in your car?'

'My water bottle.' Pero grinned.

'You're a bad liar,' I said.

'I need something to take the edge off.' Pero giggled.

'Not today. No morning beers today. Today we are going on a long walk.'

We set off in the direction of Golden Gate Bridge. It was a very beautiful day. No fog, no wind. Only the breezy blues and golds of California and her red bridge in the distance. Pero suggested we walk the bridge and head to Sausalito. He knew a nice bar on the waterfront.

The bridge was loud and the path narrow so we had to walk one behind the other. Over the roar of the traffic, with the bay sparkling beneath us, Pero said that he'd walked to the middle of the bridge a few times in some dark days and stared out at the water. He wasn't going to jump, he said, but he stood there one time really thinking about it and a passer-by noticed and walked him back to land.

'It's kind of intense living ten minutes away from the most popular suicide spot in the world.'

We kept walking and Pero kept talking. Most of it revolved around the DUI or a time he had sex with a girl. We got to the end of the bridge and clambered over one of the blue hills we had been looking at from the beach the day before. No longer blue of course now that we were right up in it. Hot, pale rocks; thick shrubs; dried-out yellow and spiky vines that may or not have been poison oak.

Pero was talking about a forty-year-old he'd had sex with from work, and another girl from the catering job. That was the only time he'd had sex with two different people, in different places on the same day. One after the catering job and the other after the nursing shift. 'Pero, I shouldn't have done it but it was very good.'

I felt afraid, clambering down the hill in the hot sun, but I couldn't place exactly what I was afraid of. There was some kind of a military checkpoint at the bottom and we were vaguely trespassing and there was the roaring suicide bridge above and Pero non-stop talking and Michael strangely silent, in a strange, unidentifiable mood, which unnerved me. I was thinking of a Jean Rhys story I'd read when we were camping, in which a woman remembered a frightening song her father used to sing: '*You're not my daughter if you're afraid of the shape of a hill, or the moon when it's growing old.*' It made me think that landscapes can be haunted and there was darkness lurking in this in-between place that we were clambering through on our way to Sausalito, something that made me cold to the bone, even in the sunshine. I could believe there were spirits in the landscape and these spirits had something to do with what might make us drink or fall in love or jump off a bridge. I told Michael. Didn't he feel something was wrong in the air here too?

'Oh donkey,' he said. 'You were born uncomfortable.'

At the military checkpoint we found a portable toilet and sink and washed our legs down.

'One time I got poison oak on my pee-pee after me

and Jenna had sex in the woods,' Pero said. 'That was one of the worst days of my life too.'

There was no way to Sausalito via the coastline. We found a road and followed it back up the other side of the hill we had just clambered down. 'I've heard I have the perfect-size penis. Not too big, not too small. But you can't always trust what people say. There was one time I told a girl that was the best blow job ever when it definitely wasn't.'

Sausalito was spooky in a different way. Paved and rich and suspicious. When we got to the main drag, I was so anxious that I needed a drink too. We made it to the place Pero had in mind: a soulless waterfront bar, where we ordered three IPAs. The beers landed on the table. We toasted Pero for making it to two p.m. Pero's hand was shaking. How long had it been that he'd lasted this long? He giggled. He didn't remember.

On the walk back along the Sausalito waterfront a glossy brown-and-white pedigree dog jumped on Pero's thighs. 'What a beautiful Bernese!' Attached to the dog was a girl. Pero asked her if she lived around here. It turned out she lived in the Presidio too, not far from him. She gave Pero the handle to her dog's Instagram and said he could walk it sometime.

None of us wanted to cross the bridge again on foot. Pero ordered us a taxi. In the car he asked the girl out via her dog's Instagram.

'Little does she know I'm a bad dog. I've got problems.'

★

Cleaning up Pero's apartment for the last time, looking for something to eat. Everything felt very far away. This can, this dirty plate. They already belonged in a past time I'd escaped.

We said goodbye at the Sienna. Pero's grandad's car was parked right next to it and there was something very sad about the sight of the two inherited vehicles together. Pero wasn't even allowed to drive his grandad's car any more. Through the windscreen I could see the Pope's bobble head still attached to the dash with his hands in the air, surely begging.

'Thank you for having us,' I said. He teared up. 'Thanks for being good *perros*. Thanks for looking after me.'

'I love you, Pero,' Michael said. He backed the Sienna out of the parking space and I watched the forlorn Pero head back to his apartment alone.

Come on, Perro! I wanted to shout out to him. If only he had a walker. Way to go, Pedro! You can do it, Bruno. Go home and don't drink. Don't do it, Dudley! I believe in you, Dudley! I believe you will be a wonderful father, Dudley!

As if he really was a dog. As if calling out to him while I left with Michael would make him listen and stop.

Lake View

'*Toe blue . . . toe blue . . . too blue . . .*'

He's gone now but I've woken up in a Lake Michigan hotel room wanting to remember one of his songs. The sun is shining on the blinding blue lake and through the windows. My sister is sleeping beside me. My older half-sister half-mother Emma with the crisp pillow over her head, who drank too much last night and now will not get out of bed or raise her head to look out upon the lake view she paid for especially to make me feel better.

Toe blue, too blue . . . How did the rest of it go? *Lake blue, lake blue. Lake open wide. I forget my love has teeth . . .*

We were sitting further up the lake years ago when he was making up the words. A late-September evening in Chicago, sharing a picnic on the concrete ledge. I was in charge of pouring the wine in little cups, otherwise he would drink the whole thing at once. The faint hill of a harvest moon rose from the lake. The geese ate the grass. A jet-ski passed. A shirtless guy jumped off the concrete and splashed into the water and Michael sang *toe blue, blue, blue* until a slight young man in a stiff-collared purple shirt and white Cuban boots clip-clopped along on the concrete shore and stood before us with a microphone, a stand and a PA system.

'Good evening, ladies and gentlemen,' he said shyly. 'My name is Rico and I will be your singer tonight.' Dark hair combed back from his pale forehead, he was like a young Latin Dracula. A woman riding a pink bike and wearing a pink helmet, pink leggings, pink shoes and a pink jacket crossed his stage. As she passed us she turned and gave a twinkling smile. The boy raised his eyes from his boots and asked us if we minded if he played a set. He said he wanted to sing in clubs but he was still learning how to interact with an audience. We clapped and he began with a sweet and shaky rendition of 'Amazing Grace'. 'Thank you, America!' he called out into the microphone. 'Stay strong and beautiful!' We clapped along and he got into the swing of things, singing a few Amy Winehouse songs while behind him the moon became whole, grew bright and lit a path across the water. By the time he got to Peggy Lee's 'Is That All There Is?' shy Rico was totally transformed, stomping and swaying, arching his eyebrows. 'Thank you, ladies and gentlemen!' he called to us between each song. We cheered and danced around because we were the only ladies and gentlemen watching his show. 'And this one is for all those courageous enough to fall in love!' He blew kisses, the lights flickered on across the downtown Chicago skyline and the frightening antennas on the Sears Tower turned blue too and billowed smoke.

Room blue, room blue. My sister seems to be in great agony. She's not, she says. She just needs more sleep. She sounds like ET gasping on a ventilator. OK, so I'll go on a walk and when I get back we'll go somewhere that isn't Navy Pier? No answer. The pier is freezing. The lake is endlessly still. Michael must be camping somewhere in Kansas by now. He is driving back to California, with his dad's old van packed with all his junk and some things that used to be our junk, to move back for good after living in a basement in Bushwick when we broke up six months ago. I wasn't so nice to him but he wasn't so nice to me, just showing up at Emma's house in Grayslake, Illinois a few days ago where I've been staying, partly to get away from living in the same city as him.

He had called, knowing that I was there, thinking it would be a good idea to stop along the way and say goodbye. I told him it was not a good idea, that of course I wanted to see him but we'd already spent all these months trying to break up, and then I hid from my phone for the rest of the day. But by the evening he was ringing the doorbell of my sister's house. Waffle barked like mad and my seven-year-old nephew Max ran to the door saying, 'Don't worry, Waffle! Michael is a good alien!'

He had a beard now. He was wearing leggings and a red T-shirt advertising a pizza place. His big brown eyes were very sad and he was frowning at me. He asked me where he'd be sleeping and I said, 'I don't know where you are sleeping, Michael. I told you not to come!' Max begged him to play *Super Smash Bros* with him straight away and I snuck upstairs where my sister was working a night shift at her newspaper job and fell asleep on the sofa beside her desk. When I woke up he was curled on the other side, turned away from me, and both of us were under one of Emma's furry pink blankets.

In the morning, a grey sky hung over all the identical clapboard houses. Michael shuffled between Emma's house and his van, sorting out his things, working through a list of tasks, looking downtrodden and glaring at me. Little Waffle followed him everywhere he went. Max followed Waffle. They were taking care of him. Michael put every item of clothing he owned through Emma's washer and dryer. I folded his clothes.

'Throw out anything you don't like,' he told me. 'Throw it all out. I don't wear clothes, clothes wear me.' Waffle lay on a pile of washed and folded clothes. Max sat beside Michael and set up a game of Pairs.

'Are you really an alien, Michael? Were you just lying when you told me that before? How old were you when I was born? Were you alive in cowboy times?'

I folded a purple shirt I'd never seen before. 'Hey, this one is kind of nice!'

Michael tore it out my hands and put an arm through a sleeve. 'I was going to look nice for you. I was going to wear a sexy outfit but then you didn't answer your phone and I got fucked up from driving sixteen hours straight!'

The next thing he needed to do was buy a camping stove for his cross-country journey home. I said I'd go with him to a place called Outdoor World, in Gurnee. Sitting in the passenger's seat, I caught a glimpse of the packed-up car in the rear-view mirror: the blue painted mattress platform; pieces of wood that had been our desk; our blanket tucked under our pillow case . . . and I did not look back there again. Ten minutes of six-lane freeway and heartbreaking silence.

'You're a terrible person,' he said eventually. 'You're evil. You're just a lost, scared girl. You need five volts to the head and river, ice, yoga.'

'That's just mean,' I said.

He thought about it. 'Fine. You're not a terrible person. Just terrible to me. Evil, et cetera.'

'Well, why the hell are you here then?' I asked.

'Because this is your last chance, donkey. This is my last-ditch declaration of love.'

'By telling me I am terrible and evil? What is the point!'

I burst into tears and he stared solemnly at the road ahead, following the final two minutes of directions to the parking lot of Outdoor World. 'See,' I said, getting out the car. 'We make each other so miserable. I can't see straight when you're around. I don't know what I think or who I am or who you are.'

'I don't care!' he said. He came around and pulled me

to his chest. 'Helen, I would rather be miserable with you than happy without you.'

Outdoor World is a huge strip mall in the style of an Old West Lodge. Aisles of hunting apparel, fishing apparel, men's apparel, sunglasses, fishing rods and reels in all the colours of the rainbow. Hooks, bait, guns, binoculars, kayaks, canoes and cuddly toys, held together in packaging covered in images of forests and waterfalls and rocky creeks. In the middle of all this was a massive fishtank sculpture, with a stuffed cougar and two stuffed deer perched on a tower of rocks above the water, where real Lake County trout swam behind the glass in their fish hell.

It took us a long time, just wading through every aisle of Outdoor World, until we finally found the very tiny section that sold camping stoves. At the checkout, he paid seventy dollars for the smallest, cheapest stove. On the wall above the exit hung a skinned grizzly bear, a skinned brown bear, a beaver, and a dozen or so stag heads on mounts.

'Humans do that to humans too, you know,' he said, gesturing to the diorama of hung dead things.

'I don't want to know,' I said to him.

'Back to sleep, sheep,' he said. 'The only way out is through God, with love and Michael.'

When we got back to the house, Max dared Michael to eat a teaspoon of salt. Michael ate the teaspoon of salt and quickly became very ill, clutching his stomach in pain and glaring at me.

'Why are you looking at me like that? I didn't dare you to eat a teaspoon of salt.'

He disappeared to have an hour-long shower, glared at me once more through a cloud of steam, and spent the rest of the evening playing *Super Smash Bros* with Max again.

'I can't bear it,' I said to Emma.

'He will leave eventually and you will miss him then, so just try and get through it, I guess.'

I curled up on the sofa again, thinking: What kind of a person eats salt because a seven-year-old dares him? What kind of a person makes such a confused and painful last-ditch declaration of love? He refuses to make sense and that's what makes him special. He lives in a world that does not accept him and that's what makes him mean. He takes up residence in people's heads, hearts and homes, invited or not invited, and I'm losing myself in his nonsense again. I cannot let him back in when I spent all these months trying to pull him out of me. I need to close the shutters and lock the doors and batten down the hatches. I cannot let him back in. I cannot let him back in . . .

I fell asleep on the sofa and woke up sometime in the early morning to him poking me sadly. 'Just one last time?' And after all that I let him in so easily. Now it was my turn to have an hour-long shower and glare at him all morning. 'Melon . . . are you going to be nice to me today? Melon, maybe if you get pregnant it will be a sign . . . Melon, can you be nice to me for twelve hours? Eleven hours? Ten hours? I just need to get an oil change on my van and then I'll go. Melon? Please?'

What is right and what is wrong? There is good and evil and blue and grey and I'm not a judge or a songwriter. Jean Rhys once holed up in a gloomy hotel and put herself on trial for ten pages. Did she believe in God? She didn't know. In love? Yes, somehow she still did.

In humanity?
No.
How can you believe in human love and not in humanity?
Because I believe that sometimes human beings can be more than themselves.

On the Sunday morning I was reading those ten pages and Michael was back in his leggings and pizza T-shirt. Grayslake, Illinois had issued a high-wind warning but Emma had the idea to try and make it to the 'werkout' dance class at Life Time gym to cheer everyone up: 'And it looks like Michael's already dressed for it!'

I said I didn't want to get sucked up in a tornado. Michael said he would drive safely. Emma rushed us to the car: 'The dance-teacher woman is just really inspiring. She lifts people up. I don't really know how to explain it. She just makes people feel good.'

Back at the six-lane intersection again, the hanging

traffic lights went loop de loop. The wind battered the shell of Emma's little car and ripped rubber from the back window. We had to stop the car on the side of the road and Michael bashed the rubber back in. There were hardly any other cars.

'Do not let go of that steering wheel, Michael!'

Cross the plains and the plains cross you. Michael driving, God was on our side. Cross Michael and God crosses you. Michael crosses the plains and you will be safe. You will get to Life Time gym, drop Max in the kids' area and make it into the exercise class, just ten minutes late. The ladies were clapping and stepping and kicking and getting low. Michael did all his own crazy moves and looked ridiculous but the ladies loved him. Emma did her own moves too, though she tried her best to follow the teacher. And I don't know how else to say it either. The woman did something and we became more than ourselves.

'I can be nice for six hours,' I told Michael outside the men's changing rooms and kissed him on the cheek. He yelped and jumped in the air.

'Thank you, Melon! I know I'm a little bit weird but I'm a catch and a half!'

Which brings me back to Jean Rhys again, who was brilliant and a nightmare and so haunted and miserable that it was a miracle she wrote anything. When she first laid eyes upon England on the boat from Dominica, she looked upon all the dirty grey water and knew in an instant all that would happen to her . . . and she carried on anyway, 'another poor devil of a human being'. It's not that we need these kinds of people to see the light. Just to know that they were born from the same world, so inhospitable to their madness, and still would not be silenced or stamped down. That is what we need . . . but this doesn't mean we have to marry them or put up with their nonsense! When Michael and I first fell in love I stubbed my toe on the step into our motel room in Santa Cruz and overnight it turned blue. We had one cigarette left but couldn't find a lighter. Stormy sea, not a soul on the boardwalk except a homeless man standing by the entrance to the arcade. He had one match left and he offered it to Michael. They huddled together and managed to get the cigarette burning. I saw a sign for a palm reader on a door. The palm shed a shadow, made the shape of a bird and took flight. 'You're a last-match kind of girl!' he said and didn't explain what he meant. But I suppose over the years there was always a last match and a way back together, and it seemed there would always be a miracle last match until there wasn't.

And so he was trying, looking handsome in his purple shirt for the last time on his last night, and we were having a taco party. Carnitas, beans, potato chips, salsa. 'We're having a taco party! We're having a last-time-I-ever-see-Michael party!'

Max was confused. 'But it will never be the-last-time-you-see-Michael party?'

Doing the motions, doing the movements. I was thinking if we had a child we could be happy. We would be poor and he would adore that child and please God don't give me a sign.

'Michael, I dare you to eat two teaspoons of salt,' Max said.

'No one is eating any more salt!'

After dinner we watched *Austin Powers*, all of us on the sofa while Emma worked her final shift for the week at her desk across from the TV. I'd eaten so much that I fell asleep in the middle and woke up to the credits rolling.

'Aunty Helen, what does "shag" mean?'

'Oh dear . . .' My head weighed a lifetime of hellos and goodbyes to Michael. Emma took Max to bed and Michael and I curled up back to sleep on the sofa again. The sleep of the dead. Angel on my pillow. The sleepiest of chests. He could be so calm and reasonable sometimes and not many people saw that. I slept so well. He made me so tired. I was still asleep when he was packing the car in the morning. I knew I should go to help him. I could not get up, could barely open my eyes again when he said he was ready to go. He carried the pile of folded washing down the stairs. I followed him to the car.

'You don't have to go today.'

But he was leaving: 'It's too hard on the heart.'

The clothes were back in his suitcase. The car

mattress bed was made up with the cuddly toy llama his mom gave him tucked neatly under our old blanket. He did that on purpose to break my heart. The packed-up Sienna pulled out, drove past three other identical drives and disappeared around the corner. Across the street, a sidewalk maple tree let go of a few last leaves.

Emma was in the kitchen when I went back inside. All the blinds were open, and the sun poured in across the floor and counters and kitchen island, which suddenly seemed so clean and bare and empty of Michael.

'Well. That was an interesting chapter,' she said. She was in a good mood because it was finally her weekend and we were going to go away for the night to stay at this hotel with the lake view. She pointed out a big bag of junk that Michael had left behind. At the top was the purple shirt. 'For god's sake.'

I sat at the table and put my head in my hands. In the next room Max had *Chucky* the TV series blaring: 'Chucky, you killed my mother. Chucky, you killed my father. When will we get this evil out of you?'

Emma opened the fridge to make herself some kind of diet cucumber wrap. Waffle waddled into the room and sat on my feet. Emma chopped up her cucumber.

'Do you miss Michael?' she asked me, or Waffle. 'Because I do.'

PART THREE

CAN I CoMe in?

Haunted House

I haven't been home in three years and my father has been dead for seven more but for some reason his briefcase is balanced on the top of the washing basket in the bathroom on my first night back at the house.

I'm brushing my teeth and stop to ask my mother what the hell it's doing there. She comes into the bathroom and seems to be just as confused. 'Maybe Allister put it there when he was here painting the skirting boards a few days ago . . . Or maybe I put it there absent-mindedly when I was cleaning . . . which would be a pretty strange thing to do.'

She laughs and heads for the toilet, as if she's still alone.

'It's crazy that the thing is still banging around. Has anyone ever gone through it?'

She shakes her head and begins to pee. 'No idea.'

'Not even you?'

'Oh no, never.'

'Really? Never? After all this time?'

'I guess I'm weird like that,' she says.

I pick up the briefcase, poor sad sack. Spent most of its life in the corner by the record player. It was a rare, encouraging sight to see my dad heading out the door in his jacket, shoes and briefcase, all similar shades of rusty brown leather. The university had forced him into early medical retirement after his time in rehab in 1996 but hired him back to teach one class a semester. Sometimes he found the courage to walk out the door, briefcase in tow, and use his office to do some marking or work on the book he never finished. Sometimes he got all dressed up in brown just to use his office for a secret place to drink. In any case, it wasn't often. I don't have many memories of him outside of the house at all. And so the briefcase stayed where it was last left, for many years, just as his shoes stayed in the basket by the front door and his leather jacket in the hallway cupboard. Just as most things in this house seem to remain eternally in the last spot where whichever beloved family member or friend or handy-craftsman Allister happened to abandon them on their way out.

'Why don't we open it now then,' I say to my mother.

'Oh no.' She flushes the toilet and quickly heads for the door. 'Not tonight, honey. Not right before bed.'

She turns off the kitchen lights, locks the front door and goes upstairs, but I feel as awake as the bright East Coast afternoon I left for good yesterday. Cool April night in the windowpane, reflecting the oppressively unchanged bathroom: basket of odd socks, plastic container of bath toys and ageing toiletries. A sewing box that was maybe last used twenty years ago beside a sandwich bag full of crusty make-up that belonged to Emma at some point. The baby bath and changing mat and bag of Babygros and white-noise sheep thing she bought for Max when he was a sleepless newborn, eight years ago. The contraption that my mother's father used to get on and off the toilet when he was staying with her before he died, back when I was living in London. A still life of left-behind life: the busy bathroom of a big family, careless with their belongings; the comings and goings of people who don't live here any more. A still life my mother is still living inside, bathing and changing and going to the toilet all alone, never thinking or wanting to move a thing.

The first thing I find inside the briefcase is a pile of very dusty baseball caps that must have been shoved in there recently as they are so disgustingly dusty and that makes no sense. But underneath, the museum of my father's briefcase is pretty much intact. There are bills, a cheque book, a comb, an Oyster card for all the times he never went to London, some unlucky student's dissertation on globalisation in Europe, and an address book containing just the addresses of wherever his siblings and children and stepchildren lived nine years ago. In a side pocket is a packet of paracetamol, half a pack of Rennie and two biros held neatly in two elastic pen holders. Memories come swirling up with the dust from the caps. *Dad, can I borrow a pen? Dad, do you have change for the bus? Dad, do you have any paracetamol?* He goes to the briefcase in the corner and bends with a sigh to get whatever I need. *Give the pen back this time. Yeah, yeah, I know.* In another side pocket is a pack of Kleenex with a couple missing. *It's OK, Helen . . . don't cry,* he says and rummages for a tissue.

I buckle up the briefcase again and fling it behind the basket. It lands sadly on the floor with the buckles facing down.

★

There are eight recessed lights in the ceiling over the kitchen table and they are way too bright. The brightest spotlight shines directly over my mother's plate during dinner. Her plate is the stage and I've been a gloomy audience these first weeks back, so her stories have been holding together our dinnertime. There is the story of her sister being forgotten at the train station in Egypt in 1973. The story of Soviet ships going down the Bosphorus when she was a child in Istanbul during the Cuban Missile Crisis. The story of the condemned Italian ship where she celebrated her tenth birthday. And then there are the stories of our family: the big falling-apart house they rented when Pandora and I were babies, when Emma and Matthew were young teenagers and my dad's children Kimber and Rachel came for weekends; when my father's drinking was at its worst and she was struggling to make ends meet writing freelance journalism. The kids ran wild and helped her look after the babies when Frank was losing his mind. The creepy house with the long corridors and locked doors and doors that opened to walls. The Hungarian furniture smugglers who owned the house and filled it with creepy artworks. The disused sauna in the basement that was full of A5 prints of those creepy artworks. The story of when my dad's first daughter, Rachel, went to live permanently with her mother and didn't see us again for ten years. The story of when my mother's first daughter, Emma, moved to London to live with her father permanently. How it broke her heart when Emma left but she didn't want to make her choose between her parents. They'd speak every afternoon after school and she'd help her with her homework. Did I know what a gift it was, she asks, to speak to Emma without anyone else interfering?

I've heard it all a thousand times but what else is there to talk about? The days here are endless and eventless and the past is everywhere, though my mother has made a quiet and cheerful life here in this village outside Bath that we ended up in randomly and where she never really belonged. Talking to students, teaching seminars, attending neighbours' exercise classes, shopping, preparing dinner – the kind of life she never had time to live when I was growing up.

It's just I had my own life too and now I don't. I had a present and now I only have a past because years of bad decisions have landed me back here indefinitely. I just don't know what to do with myself. I'm travelling up and down the stairs, crossing great distances, peeking into rooms and bags and boxes. Every time I move something there are memories hiding under memories. Then the day ends again and it is time for dinner. We eat the lovingly prepared meal-for-two, while the stories run around us, trying to catch up with one another, just how my sister chased a boy around the table when she was five and split her chin open on a pot and that is another story. My mother has told these stories so many times it seems she no longer feels them. She hasn't cried in ten years! Not since my father died and she had to hold it all together and not break down; and did I remember the time, just before the funeral, when I sat in her office, sat on her lap actually, and told her how when Dad was alive I saw him as two people – the loving dad and the addict dad and I was always angry at the both of them? But now that he was dead, I couldn't be angry. I could see them all tangled together as one and understand him.

Sometimes when she is telling me these things under the too-bright lights the mini heater by my feet melts the pale wall across from us into waves of hot air and I'm brought to tears – not just for the stories themselves but the light, the long day. The dark windows, the memories hiding under memories and too many moments from the past boiling and bubbling up, all mixed up together – needing some kind of release which happens to be out of my eyes. Now there is the story of when she was visiting me in New York a year ago. A bad dinner. Michael screaming about how no one talks about 5G while I'm crying in the pasta. The waitress gave us a couple of drooping sunflowers as we were leaving. My mum went to the bathroom and when she came out of the restaurant the scene was very dark and eerie because workers were tarmacking the street. She turned the corner to see me hitting Michael with my bouquet. The yellow petals flying in the night and me screaming: 'I hate you! I hate you! I hate you!' It was so cinematic, she tells me at the table, as I begin to cry. 'All the petals flying against the dark tarmac night as you both stood under a lamp post.' It was so beautiful and it happened a hundred years ago to people we don't know.

★

What is the point of doors when they're always open? The bathroom, the bedrooms, Mum's office. Passing my mum's bedroom, a gust of wind throws the door shut. White wooden door with a smile-shaped handle; a shaft of sunlight runs diagonally across it. Spooky memory: smoke wafting out of the door in the daytime. The doors were only closed when my dad was secretly drinking or recovering from drinking behind one. Spooky memory ends. I notice some scraps in the keyhole and find a pencil to manoeuvre them out. On the first scrap are some letters in a child's handwriting. *CaNe?* The second scrap is wedged further in. I have to poke around with a pencil for a while. It emerges dusty and crinkled, the same handwriting with the sweet, wonky words: *CAN I CoMe in?*

*

Inside these rooms there must be something to explain something but I just don't know how to find it. *CAN I CoMe in?*

My mum tells me that on the day we moved into this house the movers were a bunch of drunks who had only fifteen boxes between them. She says that she would fill the boxes, the movers would dump the stuff at the new house and come back with the fifteen empty boxes. She says that when God packs up her life at the end of it all he will probably be drunk too. Why did they only have fifteen boxes? Why did no one go out and get some more? A box shortage in the South West, she says. Some weird thing. She says my dad was drunk of course. 'All he could think about was the stupid gecko. What was his name again? Gordon the Gecko? He was sat in the passenger seat holding the tank with Gordon the Gecko inside it. Every time I'd brake he'd scream: "Don't do that! Gordon won't make it! Gordon won't make it!" It drove me insane! Of course Gordon didn't make it. More tragedy . . . Then we discovered that the drunks had just emptied boxes and furniture. In every room just mountains of junk. It was impossible to move stuff to make room for anything. I don't know how we did it. I don't know how we did anything. That same day the gecko died and Frank went missing. Later that week you started school and it was your fifth birthday. You were very sad, I remember. Yes, it was your fifth birthday and you were very sad.'

★

Gordon the Gecko. He crawled between my hands, up walls and under ceilings. With feet as dry as rocks and eyes dark like the insides of rocks. I stroked his back with a finger, all the way from his head to his tail, and he stayed so still. Those tiny scales. Dad brought back bugs from the pet shop, clicking little black things, and we poured them in the tank. Gordon stuck out his tongue and turned from rock to river to erase them. Gordon on his back in the tank by the new front door the day I turned five. The sad tank with the twigs and the leaves and the sticks. But how could something that was living and ate living things die by just sitting in a car? No matter how many ways my mother or brothers or sisters tried to explain it, I just couldn't get my head around it. His little heart went out. There was a lot of bumping on the move. The lizard didn't know what was happening. He fell asleep. He was old anyway. Moves are stressful. I just can't hear any more about the gecko right now. Every answer just left a big hole in my head. Poor Gordon, poor Gordon.

★

The house sits amongst a row of cottages at the foot of an Iron Age hill fort. I've started walking up the hill whenever the day or the past gets under my skin. It's a steep fifteen-minute walk to the top and it feels good to get the feet moving. One two, one two. Climbing uphill instead of existing uphill. The trees rustle, the wind moves the thoughts on, the Neolithic villagers battle and pray to the goddess Sulis of the springs, with which this hill is bursting. And spring is in the air too . . . though it's technically early summer. Hopeful breezes and slices of blue between the clouds. At the top of the hill I'm happy to be alive and have a mother down the hill who is annoying and caring for me. I feel gusty and sentimental. A field of long grass, rushes of green love for everyone around to be loved, close to the cloudy heavens and the wet footsteps of ancient people. Back down the hill and across the road I hear of a man who dug a hole in his back garden and refused to get out. According to an article published in the *Bath Chronicle* the man had been digging the hole for weeks. The article says that emergency services fixed a crane over the hole in an attempt to go down and get him. In the end, though, the crane wasn't necessary. 'The incident was resolved and the man got out of the hole of his own accord.'

★

'You remember falling in the pond at Frank's rehab?'

The plate is shining tonight. Roast chicken that looks like fried chicken, just shining.

'Yes, of course I remember! You know I remember!'

She carries on anyway. I was three and my brother jumped in to save me. She tells me Kimber was always very proud of that. She had been at a family meeting inside and he came through the door carrying me, totally soaked. They had to wrap me up in her coat because I didn't have any dry clothes. 'You remember that?'

I tell her I remember being put in one of Dad's smoky jumpers.

'Hm,' she says, 'I'm pretty sure it was my coat. And you were so upset when we were leaving. You wouldn't stop crying. We thought it was because you missed your dad but eventually worked out that you were afraid he was going to fall in too and no one would be around to save him.'

'I just really remember wearing one of Dad's jumpers and the smoky smell and the sleeves dragging across the carpet of his room.'

'And that you thought he was going to fall in?'

'I guess so.'

'Well anyway . . . It was a big deal for me, finally getting him to rehab. I felt like if I didn't do something he was going to try and kill himself again. It lasted three months and there was therapy and morning groups and family meetings. It was hard for him at first; he didn't think he should be there with all the addicts. He didn't even believe he was an addict. Funny how addiction makes people's perceptions so skewed. If you're as smart as he was, it becomes too easy to talk yourself out of anything. Seeing how addicts did this from the outside taught him a lot, though. I remember Frank telling me a story from one of his morning groups. There was an alcoholic guy who was furious at his ex-girlfriend because he said she'd punched his fist with her jaw. Frank said it took a huge amount of persuading and arguing for the group to get him to admit that, maybe, he'd moved his own fist a little. That it was his fault. Frank thought it was amazing. He couldn't believe it. And I said: "Frank! You never admit that anything is your fault. You would never even admit that you had a drinking problem!" He was so humiliated being there with the thieves and the addicts, but I swear it bought him eighteen more years. He learned a lot about addiction. And when he came out, he was full of ideas and energy. So optimistic. Right away he started working on his research. He was going to put forward a paper on addiction. It was wonderful to see him excited about his work again. For so long, the depression and all the rest of it had prevented him from doing that. It was such a shame, someone so brilliant . . . But before he went back to work, the university called me into a meeting and told me they didn't want him there any more. They said: "You are now going to persuade him to leave his job." I told them no. "How could I do that? He's pulling his life together! He has the new research project about addiction! Don't try and get rid of him by trying to break him!" But that's what they did, humiliating him in all sorts of ways. Sending colleagues in to assess how he taught, gathering negative feedback, all sorts of institutionalised bullying. It was incredibly painful. I'll never forget it . . . He started drinking again that summer. He had big plans to stay sober but every time there was a knock he drank. First it was just that he was fragile, then it became a pattern. Some years they were infrequent enough that you forgot. Some years it was very frequent. I don't know how we got through.'

She stops talking to take a sip of wine.

'At rehab they tell you to look at yourself in a mirror without judgement. Without escape or justifying. Just to look. I try to do that. I learned. Why suffer? Or no. We have to suffer. That is being alive. Whenever he came back and set himself back up as the father of the family, and we let him, you would look at me like I was a traitor. What could I do? I couldn't let him be homeless. Couldn't let him be one of those homeless people outside Waitrose. I was carrying so much sorrow and trying not to let you kids into my feelings. My heart was breaking all the time. But it's better than having no heart.' She cuts a piece of chicken and cheerfully places a forkful in her mouth. 'Heartbreak is not so bad,' she says, nodding and chewing. 'But a walled-up heart . . . Why stay suffering?'

★

Do not move stones, writes Sappho in the book by the toilet. Virginia Woolf writes, *Stop sloshing around in your own emotions!* The Tao-te-Ching says in all sorts of ways: *Let things be! Don't try to control them!* The day feels like a cool cool blanket, mist over the valley. I meet my old friend Theo and we walk in the woods. He's living with his parents for the summer too, recovering from a breakdown. The sun is about to set and the woods are glowing. A group of young brown cows are gathered in the middle of a field. Their coats the same golden brown as the tree trunks in the woods behind us. The sun disappears behind the hill and Theo parts the cows with his arms outstretched. His shirt is the same colour as the cows, the colour of the woods. The cows fall away obediently. Theo who is depressive and loves cowboys and looks like a cowboy in his shirt and listens to cowboy music and can sing like a cowboy but has never been to America. I follow his path and the bull stares me down.

'I'm scared!'

'Don't look the bull in the eye,' he says.

'Really?'
'Ha. Nah.'
It's a fresh day. A day that got dusted. A misty English day. 'I feel mentally ill today. I don't know.'
'If anyone knows, it's me,' Theo says.

★

At a charity bookshop attached to an old church in the next village I find a one-pound copy of Virginia Woolf's *A Haunted House* amongst a bookshelf of paperback thrillers. 'Whatever hour you woke there was a door shutting,' the story begins. It is a ghost story that is more of a love story. A ghostly couple wandering around the house of a living couple, opening and closing doors, looking for something. Floors creak, the wind blows, apples roll in the loft, the rain beats 'Safe! Safe! Safe!' and the ghostly couple are drawn apart and back together – searching while the living couple listens. And by the end of the three-page story, the ghosts find it, stooping with their lamp over the sound sleepers: 'The light in the heart.'

★

Knock on the door. *CAN I CoMe in?* Dad sits at the table. Outline of a dad. As present in the kitchen as the smoke is. He put my hair into plaits. Rumpelstiltskin, Rumpelstiltskin, turn this straw into gold! He sits at the table and he reads a mystery novel. He sits and he screams down the phone to Lucy in Massachusetts. He sits at the table and he disagrees articulately with something Mum says. He sits and he smokes and he appears and disappears in puffs. *What are you thinking?* Mum is always asking. *What the hell was I thinking?* she is always announcing. No answer. He sits at the table with the curtains closed on his face. With the curtains closed on his agony. He can't speak, he smokes, he eats the delicious meals he cooks, he leaves his cigarette in the ashtray and it burns into a cone of ash. He sits at the kitchen table until the sun goes down and then he goes to bed.

★

I killed Juliet! I killed Juliet! My father was sleep-talking on the sofa. *I fucking killed her, OK?*

This was disturbing but not out of the ordinary. I knew at nine years old that he had once had a bad break-up with a woman called Juliet and that she was still alive. More disturbing was that he wasn't wearing his glasses.

Dad, I poked him. *You should go to bed.*
I fucking killed her, OK?
Dad!
He opened his glasses-less eyes, which were so huge

suddenly. They traced a circle around the room. Whatever they were seeing was not the TV, or the wooden beams, or the green chair, or the glass door to the hallway, or me. When they got to the carpet they closed again. His head fell back and knocked the wall behind him. His eyes opened and he grumbled some spooky nonsense I couldn't understand, before heaving himself off the sofa, putting each foot in a slipper and making his slow way out the room and down the hallway.

Get to bed. It's late, he said when he got to the door of his bedroom, becoming himself again. He left his door a crack open. Through the crack of green darkness I could hear him getting into bed. Creak, creak and in a few minutes he was snoring. I crept up to the door, twisted the smile-shaped door handle, and quietly closed it.

★

My brother Kimber calls: 'What are you writing? Dad isn't the main character any more, is he? I think it's time for you to write about something else. I think you have exhausted this subject. Make someone up now. Isn't that what writers are supposed to do. It's just getting a bit weird.'

★

He was taking a long time to answer the door and when he finally did the first thing I noticed was that he wasn't wearing his slippers.

I'm not feeling well, he said. Two feet in socks creaked slowly back up the stairs.

I had the sudden urge to clean the house and bake cookies. Four p.m. Eleven years old. School today, school tomorrow. Through the back-door window, the garden had already become purple shadows. Pandora went to the toilet and I put on a Sarah Vaughan CD. Her voice was running water, washing the sad afternoon away. How to make cookies? Sugar, butter . . . I measured and poured and mixed, all this while my sister was still on the toilet and by the time she got off I was already bored of cooking. *What are you doing?* she asked. *Making cookies. What does it look like?* Her smile fell on the floor somewhere. *No, Helen. We're not allowed to use the oven.* I threw the wooden spoon across the kitchen. Some sticky mixture slapped against a cupboard. *What's wrong with you, you freak!* she said to me. *You ruined it!* I screamed back. She stomped upstairs and I banged the spoon around the kitchen for a while. A bottle fly emerged as if from a hole in the air and buzzed around my head. It had my sister's same annoying, concerned face, saying: *You ruined it! You ruined it! You threw a spoon when your sister needed a cuddle. You're a freak!*

I brought the mixing bowl of sugar and butter into the TV room. She was lying under a blanket on the pea-green sofa. *Move then.* We ate the mixture until we felt sick. And then with some kicking and scratching found a way for us both to be comfortable while also both stretching out on the sofa.

Sometimes we were just like cats. Like our two cats Pongo and Perdy. Pongo was edgy and could not be held. Perdy was soft, always purring. But we'd find them cuddled up together, side by side. Heads tucked, furry cheek on furry heart. I loved our cats. How could we ever have had a dog? A dog would have been neglected. We had to be cats too.

*

Safe! Safe! Safe! The pulse of the house beats nightly. The room opposite my bedroom beats nightly. The study my dad never used as a study. A door opening? A door shutting? The room with all the research for the book he never wrote in boxes. With the old mahogany desk he never used filled with letters and photos and mysteries. The room in which he hid and drank. The room he died inside when I was at college in California. The spare room, the sad room, the scary room, the room we just chuck stuff we don't want inside. The room that becomes a haunted bin for unwanted things. My dead grandad's suits and dead dad's old suits hanging on a rail. And boxes and boxes of his research and clippings. And my old clothes and my brothers' and sisters' old clothes and Max's old Babygros in dusty bin bags that fall apart when you touch them. An unopened box of things from when I was living in London. And a travel cot and basket of cuddly toys and my grandad's wheelchair. The room opposite my room that I avoid and turn away from when I walk up the stairs. After Max was born he and Emma stayed in that room for the summer, before they moved to Chicago. Max was always waving in the air. Emma's mother-in-law, visiting from Chicago, felt a presence and told the presence, kindly, to leave. Emma's partner saw a book floating above the desk. Max at age four told me he saw a man with white hair walking down the stairs.

'He has white hair?'
'Yeah! And he is wearing a trash bag.'
'Wait, what? What colour is his hair?'
'And he is wearing a Ghostbuster pack.'
'Oh, so you saw a Ghostbuster?'
'Yeah!'

★

My oldest brother Matthew says that when he's anxious he can't stop talking. He's visiting for a few days, sitting on the green sofa drinking from a two-litre bottle of Diet Coke, telling me about his couples therapy. He says it's actually going well. He's never done any therapy before. They sit there with this woman and he talks and his wife talks and they realise all the ways in which they have been misunderstanding each other, how much they cherish their little family and that what they want is the same thing – to be happy together. 'Oh and then we get into the deep-roots bullshit of why we are the way we are.' He had a hard time growing up. Mum was always crying and he was the one she went to when everything was too much. One time, he tells me, when we were living at the old house, she was away and my dad was drunk, sitting at the kitchen table 'looking like a crazy motherfucker, just holding this kitchen knife and talking to himself'. Matthew mimes holding a big kitchen knife with one hand and makes a face to match. He takes a big swig of Coke from the bottle, the way he used to drink the beers he doesn't any more. 'I guess I was the oldest,' he says. 'But I was only seventeen. I brought you girls into the bathroom, and we locked the door and we could hear him shouting and talking to himself.' And as Matthew says this, it's like I remember it: all of us crammed inside the bathroom of the big house on the Wellsway, even though I don't remember the bathroom of the big house on the Wellsway. I am two or three. I can hear a racket in the kitchen and a crazy man's voice saying: *I'd get away with it! I could fucking do it! I could get away with it!* But no . . . that is not my dad's voice. That is the voice of Michael's schizophrenic cousin at his time-share cabin in the Poconos two years ago. Brian's thirtieth birthday. Brian had a meltdown after twenty bottles of Bud Light and a toke from Michael's spliff. Michael and I locked ourselves in the bedroom while Brian shouted and banged and clanged around downstairs. 'I'd get away with it. I could get away with it . . .' And from the racket that came up the stairs of the time-share cabin it did sound like he had already murdered someone and was chopping him up and trying to fit the body in the bin to get away with it. Somehow I fell asleep next to Michael, waking up every so often with the murderous racket coming in and out of dreams and reality. In the morning, braced for a bloody mess, we discovered that the kitchen was immaculate. The bangs and the clangs all through the night had been the sound of Brian psychotically cleaning up. The ten-dollar cake we bought him was resting on top of all the bottles in the bin. 'Why did you throw out your cake, Brian?' Michael asked him. Brian said: 'Because I breathed all over it.'

My brother is still talking. He says a friend of his came over in the end. 'This big guy.' The big friend squared up to my dad, told him the kids were leaving, and then we all left. Where did we go? Matthew doesn't remember. Only that my dad looked like a crazy motherfucker. Holding a kitchen knife? Sharpening a knife? About to start chopping vegetables? About to cut up a birthday cake?

'I'd get away with it!' someone says inside my head. 'I'd get away with it . . .'

★

My mother and I are becoming more and more stuck in the past. So what is the point? Something to talk about? Just something to do. Something that must be done? She teaches and talks to students and writes about Istanbul in the 1960s in a room blooming with Turkish tulip patterns, in a chair by the window, right on the path. I sit by the window on the floor above. It rains, it pours. The postman knocks, the children walk by on their way to school. The view out the window remains always green. The children walk by again at three thirty on their way back from school. Through the window they can see my mother typing in her chair – a view that every child who has walked past this house on the way to school has had for thirty years at nine in the morning and three thirty in the afternoon until eternity. From up here they sound like my sister and me twenty years ago. They could be Iron Age children on their way up their sacred hill. All those damp ancient people, praying to the goddess Sulis to bring back the sun! It has been raining for two weeks straight. My mother and I bump into each other in the kitchen. The ceiling is leaking again. In 1999 this kitchen extension was built over a well. Builders poured concrete over the well and covered the concrete in tiles. While they were building the back wall they disrupted a spring. The newly built wall collapsed in the middle of the night with a great sound. They tried to funnel out the spring and rebuilt the wall and the wall fell down and they tried to funnel out the spring some more. At the end of all this someone thought it would be a good idea to fit a flat roof to a kitchen extension that sat at the bottom of a very damp hill in a very rainy country. So for the next twenty years, no matter how many times my parents hired Allister to try and fix it, there was a spring in the cupboards and there was rain falling from the ceiling and now Allister is undergoing treatment for bowel cancer and I don't think it will be long now before the kitchen is just sucked back under. The kettle boils and I say to my mum: 'All this rain is getting under my skin. I can't think straight. I am just sloshing about in emotion!'

'Well, what am I supposed to do! Poor Allister is too sick to come look at the roof right now.'

'Can't you find someone else to look at it?'

'No. Allister is the only one who knows what to do.'

'But it's driving me crazy!'

She shrugs and says: 'You have to feel things. If you don't feel them then you lose them and you end up like me, just floating. This weird person who hasn't cried in ten years.'

Another drip falls on the counter.

★

Forty days of rain? It could be . . . it certainly feels like it. Emma and Max are here for July. Max wants to feed the statue in the garden. He thinks the statue was once a real girl who was turned to stone because she didn't share. He thinks that because that's what I told him when he wouldn't share. He's eight now and we've been feeding the statue in the evenings. He prepares the plate at night. Tonight, a strawberry, some chocolate buttons and two cocktail sausages. 'How will she eat if she's a statue? Will she always be a statue? Do witches still exist? Where did the witch live, Aunty Helen? Did the witch live close by?'

And we leave it out for her to enjoy while we're sleeping. But Max has not been sleeping! He has jet-lag and hates sleeping anyway. He's still awake and hungry at six a.m. so Emma makes him a crumpet. He's so tired he's hallucinating. 'Did you put sleeping powder on my crumble?' he asks her. Then he says: 'I thought you were Grandma then. I thought you were the tooth fairy . . . and I haven't even seen the tooth fairy before.'

He sleeps all morning and I go to the statue to dispose of the food before he wakes up. The plate by the statue is now empty apart from the two cocktail sausages which have tiny bites all over. There is a wasp on the end of one, wiggling and nibbling. And it makes me think of something I don't remember. Of walking in on an insect doing something vaguely human and shameful. Like the time a seagull ate my cheese-and-pickle sandwich at school and then was hanging around the playground all lunchtime with pickle on its beak, no idea that it had pickle on its beak or what pickle was. And my Grandad John, with crumbs in his beard. My mother with food on her pyjamas. My father's mother with salmon on her face in the retirement home in Philadelphia, the last time I saw her before she died. She kept telling me I was pale, asking me if I was married and saying I was an old maid. Kimber, Pandora and I asked the nurses if we could wheel her out for a walk. It was a warm October day, much warmer than it was supposed to be, and the retirement home was so depressing and airless, decorated with red plastic leaves. She was ninety-seven and barely alive and we wanted her to feel what it was like outside, with the yellow trees and the sunshine. We wheeled her out and I found a real leaf on the ground and handed it her. I wanted her to remember that she wasn't just a body plugged into a hot stuffy building, but something of this earth like the leaf in her hands. Of course I didn't tell her any of that. Her face when I handed her the leaf was far too frightening and cold. She didn't seem to enjoy being outside. The grounds were hilly and it was an effort to push her. Pandora and Kimber were hovering behind me very anxiously at the top of a hill. I was tempted just to let her go, ride down the hill and into the pond, feel life for a second before she died, and they must have felt it. Kimber took over pushing the wheelchair. 'Do you like the walk, Granny?' he asked. 'It's fine,' she said. On the way back in we stopped her wheelchair at a display of real pumpkins at the entrance and I took a picture. She didn't understand why I was taking a picture and nor did I. She said, 'Pretty soon you won't be able to tell the difference between me and the pumpkins.'

Now there is a wasp eating a sausage and a Chekhov

story about a man who is afraid of life and doesn't understand it, who sees a beetle in the grass 'which was born yesterday and understands nothing', and in the beetle he sees that life is only fear, and in the terror he sees himself. And in the wasp I see the pumpkin and in the empty plate Max sees a statue who comes alive at night to eat strawberries and chocolate, which is nothing to be afraid of, we tell him. The witch is long gone. There's nothing to be afraid of at all!

★

'I'm so happy!' Max says at the top of the hill, taking in the view for the first time. 'I'm so happy I don't know what to feel.'

'Maybe you feel free?'

'Yeah! I feel free. But I don't want to say how I feel. Because then I will be confused.'

'Because words kill the feeling?'

'I don't know how to feel because I don't feel anything! And if I try to feel something I don't know what to feel. I will be confused and I don't want to be confused.'

He laughs and falls back on the grass.

'OK, I'm gonna roll down the hill now.'

★

Fry garlic for two minutes, pour two cans of chopped tomatoes in the pan with butter, add an onion chopped in half, add a big chunk of butter and then leave it to simmer down for a few hours. Me and Emma have gone off cooking apart from this pasta. There is something about the pot gently bubbling and the kitchen smelling lightly of garlic and the fact it requires just five minutes of preparation and only one second of chopping. It makes us feel homely and nurtured and calms the edges with the minimum effort. It unhaunts the day. We drink quite a bit of wine while it simmers down.

Emma says something about feeling bad about Max being an only child. My mother says she feels responsible. That she worries she put her and Matthew off having more children by how crazy it was when we were young.

'No, Mum,' Emma says. 'It's not that. It's because it's just too hard. I can barely cope with one. I don't know how you did it.'

'Well, I only managed because you children were so wonderful. But I will always feel so guilty about what we put you through.'

'Don't feel guilty, Mum!' I say.

And Emma says, 'I guess we're a guilty bunch.'

After dinner we drink quite a bit more wine.

'You came out crying and Pandora came out smiling,' Emma tells me after Mum has gone to bed. 'Oh, but you were such little munchkins. When Mum had to go to work, she told me to make sure that Frank didn't drop you when he was drunk. I was ten so I took it to heart. I'd fight him and lock you and Pandora in my room with me. The nanny Polly was gone then,' she said. My other half-sister Rachel was gone too. 'And I was glad about that because they were my competition. Now I had you all to myself. It was my one role in life to protect you.' She gets up and helps herself to another bowl of pasta. 'Oh, I just love it when you make this pasta,' she says.

★

My mother is turning seventy and five of her six children and stepchildren have made it from their corners of the world to see her. This is a house that needs people in it. I'm going up and down the stairs just to feel how happy I am that people are in it. Pandora and Max sitting on the sofa, playing on their separate Nintendos. Emma working in Pandora's room. Mum and Matthew discussing an Ottoman translation in the kitchen. Rachel making tea. I go sit at the window and Max comes up to read the pranks section of the *Beano* in the corner of the room.

'Aunty Helen, do you have any onions up here?'

'No. No onions.'

I'm reading a new poem inspired by an old poem about the colour green. The radio says that music improves pigs' moods. Unprecedented numbers of fish and insects are dying in rivers across the globe. There has been a fourteen per cent rise in the number of postal workers being attacked by dogs. Green green this is the summer we are even more depressed by the weather. When Max asks if he can speak to Michael I don't know what to say.

'Why have you become a statue?' Max asks. 'Did you not share? Were you mean to the witch?'

Green is the colour of witches and summer and missing Michael.

Max gets up and stands in the doorway. 'Aunty Helen?' he says. 'Why are you living the same day all over again?'

★

Bonnie Raitt is singing about flies in the kitchen, the family has flown and the last of the summer flies are spiralling up the stairs and buzzing all over the world just to drive me crazy.

I find a Post-it on a notebook from when I was living with Michael:

> *The things I threw at Michael:*
> *an orange, some keys, this pen, this Post-it.*

There are flies in the kitchen, spiralling and knocking their tiny heads against all the windows in this house, over and over.

'Oh, it's fine. They'll die soon.'
'But will they die, Mum? Won't they just keep birthing maggots?'

The things I throw at the flies: a bread knife. A chopping board. A newspaper. A roll of paper towels.
'Stop doing that!'
Matthew, back in Scotland, is on the phone to our mum on loudspeaker and asks her what's going on.
'Helen is throwing inappropriate things at the flies!'
Matthew laughs and then goes back to telling her about his couples therapy session.
She's still paying for his therapy because she still feels responsible. We're a guilty bunch. She asks him how much she needs to send him and he says sixty pounds for this week. 'If you could throw in another five thousand that would save the marriage for sure.'
Mum's laugh glides up the stairs with me and then, for a long moment, fills the whole house.
But oh my god! The flies! They escape me!

★

'Mum?'
'Yes, honey?'
'Why is the calendar still on August 2018?'
'Is it? I guess I like the pattern.'
'Why does the shower still not work?'

'I don't know.'

'Why is the toilet five hundred years old? What is that smell? Why is there a weird smell all over the kitchen? Why is the ceiling still leaking? Why is that contraption that John used to get off the toilet still in the bathroom? How long have all these birthday cards been on display? Why are the lights so bright? Why is your chewing so loud? Can you eat with your mouth closed? Why do you always have to go to the toilet with the door open? Can you just close the door. It stinks.'

'Helen! Please! For god's sake! Stop it!'

★

Open the door to Dad's spooky office for two minutes, open the door for ten minutes. Unhaunt a house for a few hours. Peek into the bulging drawers of Dad's antique desk: letters, scraps of paper, my grandmother's heirloom silver comb . . . scary, scary, scary.

Put the clothes and toys and tat and stained duvet in new bin bags. Put the piles and years and years and years of my dad's sociological research laboriously charting the UK becoming a privatised bargain basement for foreign investment into boxes. Put years and years of relevant newspaper clippings in bin bags too. Along with receipts and bus tickets and bills. Find an article he wrote and put it in a frame. Find a leaflet for an anti-Vietnam protest and put it in a frame. Write down interesting findings on a piece of paper. Lose the piece of paper in all the mountains of paper. Take the very heavy bin bags down the stairs. When Mum says that is not the best way to carry paper, tell her it's too late. Tell her go get the car. Have a very hard time carrying the bags to the car in the rain. Drive to the recycling centre and park badly, annoying all the men at the dump. At the skip, tell the research and clippings: Well done, at least you tried. You had a good go. Thank you for paying attention to what the Neocons were plotting thirty years ago which has made trains so expensive and this country so sad and broken today. Even though there was nothing you could do to stop it and it never made it into a book. Good job, Dad. At least you cared. At least you were handwriting research and cutting up articles and paying attention. When Mum takes big piles in her hands and just chucks them in the skip without saying anything, tell her: 'No! Don't do it like that! You'll regret it and feel guilty. Say goodbye to the paper and well done, Frank.'

She looks at me like I'm crazy and just keeps chucking them away in big piles: 'It's raining.'

★

'Your father always supported me. He wasn't threatened by my success, he was a good person, he made us a home. He made it so nice here. Jazz in the evenings, delicious meals. He taught me how to make a home and a comforting atmosphere. He needed a home to survive. He used to say: "I wrap my family around myself and that's how I survive." That made me feel like, oh great, so I'm a blanket. But it was the first home I had. The pulse of the house beat soundly, until it didn't. Until it was a hell or he made me feel like a blanket. He made a home, until he didn't. That's just the way it was.'

★

Inside my dad's old desk there are a few organised drawers with things like envelopes and writing paper and elastic bands and paper clips in labelled tins. There are a few jumbled drawers filled with old photographs, letters from family from his college years up to the nineties. His father admonishing him for going on strike in protest against the war in Vietnam when he was a sophomore at Harvard, his sister telling him about her college friends and the music she was listening to, his brother writing about the argument he had with their father: *It doesn't matter what I do. My father will always despise me.*

Many letters from family and friends asking how London is. Wondering if he is ever going to come visit? Congratulating him on his sudden engagement to his first wife. Congratulations on your first son! Congratulations on your baby daughter! Etc. etc. *I miss you, brother. Please write back soon.*

And then every so often I come across a little piece of shame or spark of hope that he must have just shoved in the drawers over the years, when he could have just thrown them away . . .

A note from teenage Kimber writing that he has decided not to see him until he has not drunk for six months. *I would have been a lot happier if I had done this earlier. Love Kimber x (PS. This letter was very hard to write.)*

A note from my mother saying she is taking the kids away from the house. *I hope you come to your senses before you push away everyone who loves you. You deserve better than the plan the addict in you has made for you.*

Countless addiction pamphlets and worksheets: How do you weather the blowing blues? Do you have the creepy-crawlies? We imagine recovery as sailing alone on a little boat on water. When we get run down, tired and exhausted our water level is lower and we are more likely to crash into rocks. Know your rocky waters! Raise the water level! Avoid whirlpools! Wear a life jacket!

A file on the police report and legal proceedings after my mother pressed charges for violent behaviour on 12 September 2001.

A file on the Martin Luther King talk he did at my primary school.

A letter from an outraged neighbour after a drunken argument about the bins.

A file on his Safe Routes campaign to get speed bumps along the road to school.

Another file (stolen) on a farmer's campaign to remove the speed bumps. *Sign and pass on*, written on the front in someone else's handwriting.

One page in an otherwise empty notebook with a week's achievements:

> *Friday – Saw therapist, shared at AA meeting, saw friends*
> *Saturday – Took children horse-riding, cooked nice dinner*
> *Sunday – Went for a long walk with children, calmed Helen's tantrum*
> *Monday – Calmed Helen, walked children, saw doctor, dealt with finances*
> *Tuesday – Retrieved belongings, prepared lecture*
> *Wed – Prepared lecture*
> *Thurs – Gave lecture, saw counsellor*
> *Fri – Saw John*
> *Sat –*

A printout of a Pablo Neruda poem with the heading: 'How long is a man's life?' The intro to Tracy Chapman's 'Fast Car' in his handwriting.

A letter from my mother's ex-husband, telling him to never hit his daughter again.

Letters from his ex-wife on why nine-year-old Rachel has decided not to see him any more.

A letter from my father to my mother when she had thrown him out the house for a summer. *When I wake up in the morning I ask myself is it worth being alive today?*

And every day since I have started with this question some miracle has occurred to let me know it is worth being alive that day. Yesterday it was talking to you. This morning I heard the robin sing.

My mum's writing in a small purple reporter's notebook jammed at the back of the bottom drawer: *I live by the fantasies I give my children.*

Five pages of a journal from August 1997, handwritten on lined paper: *Another broken night plagued by raging anxieties . . . Again a fearful night . . . The night was mainly fear and fog . . . my fears coming raging after me . . . suffering, remorse, abandonment of responsibility, thoughts of death, the peace of the grave, self-flagellation, etc. . . . the paranoia, the need to escape, the inability to get things done, the pressure of what will happen to me, the oncoming disaster, the further stress of trying to juggle too many balls, that I am not going to make it, that I can't pull it off . . . the dread of failure and inadequacy . . . the panic and guilt . . . Fear takes over and I am frozen . . . The main thing is to keep going, make sure I do something every day . . . I will persevere . . . Today I must persevere . . . Well, a pretty bad day yesterday . . .*

★

I show the things I've found in the desk to my mum and she responds with things she's already told me.

'You know it was Jonathan, your Aunt Elizabeth's husband, who said it was a genetic thing that made him predisposed to not being able to stop drinking, like everyone else in his family.'

'I know, Mum! You said this yesterday.'

'Well, I don't know when I'm repeating myself.'

'It was yesterday!'

'OK, well I have an answer for that. You show me a new thing and I come back with a response from my own story. I wrap my narrative around myself and that's how I survive! That's my blanket and I need you to shake it up. But I don't know what you want to hear from me or not so I will just shut up and you can ask me questions if you want to know something.'

'I don't want to silence you. I just want you to stop repeating yourself.'

'I don't know when I'm repeating myself!'

I sigh and realise I am sounding just like my dad. Little criticisms of Maureen while she tries to hold it together and make a living and make conversation at dinner. Maureen, you said you would stop working an hour ago. Maureen, you already said that. Or in a page from 8 August: *Maureen has built a big wall between us. She has her reasons. It is the only way she knows how to respond to my relapse and depression and withdrawal – she carries on and does so on a basis that she must make decisions for herself and by herself (and the children which are always included in her definition of herself), however the result of this is for me to see the division in the same way. Ultimately I am on my own. My children have been taken from me before.*

His voice is in the house again. American accent with

a slightly anglicised twang. Elegant and full of sighs, all the precise words lined up, looking all depressed and neat.

★

3 August 1997

So I got through the night without taking a pill, an improvement each day, and managed to sleep a fair amount even if it was rather broken. Coming downstairs this morning the downstairs hallway looked like an art gallery. This was because I finally got around yesterday afternoon to putting Helen and (mainly) Pandora's pictures on the wall. I had sorted through them the day before – they had been sitting in a collected pile on the kitchen floor, accumulating since Christmas! It still felt like a chore at the time as I had to get Maureen to look through them which meant getting her away from her computer for ten minutes. Then I tried to get the girls to help me pick them out, which involved them wanting to stick Blu Tack everywhere, Pandora writing all over one of her pictures, both of them eventually getting bored and going upstairs, running away and screaming every time they saw me – in other words being very silly. We also watched bits of War and Peace *in the middle of all this, mainly because I wanted to see the battle scenes and couldn't remember the plot. So I had to explain to Helen who was French and who was Russian and why the uniforms were* all mixed up and which ones were the goodies and who were the baddies, all of which only she actually wanted to know.

At the end of all this when I finally pried Maureen away from her computer to help get the girls' dinner she remarked at what a good mood the girls were in and how they had obviously enjoyed the afternoon spent with me, even though, as indicated above, it had mainly involved me telling them what they couldn't do. The moral of the story I guess is that it is attention that matters rather than what you do and I had not given them much recently because I have been so self-absorbed. They really were quite happy in the evening. Helen especially but Pandora as well, affectionate and wanting to be with me at least when Maureen wasn't in the room.

So this morning the hallway looks really nice and cheerful and I managed to get the blackboard hung up as well so the mess is off the kitchen table and the hallway door. The hall is very colourful and the pictures do make the house look more like a home. Pandora's 'egg period' is particularly good, but there's a lot of interest in many of them. Just need some more from Helen since her artwork is also very good and interesting and full of love and joy.

So today I will at least get the bathroom cabinet up and put in a couple of flowering plants in the bed outside since the order and homeliness that results does pick up my mood and makes me feel less under a cloud and more in control at least of my own home.

★

I have a dream that all the furniture and belongings we ever threw away turns up at the front door, wanting to be let back in. I have another dream that I find Michael collapsed under a desk. He is supposed to be working at the computer but he's collapsed instead. My instinct is to kick him further under the desk and do his work for him. He needs help but I don't want him to get fired! If he gets fired he will lose his job and be even worse off and that thought keeps me working at the desk with my feet resting by his collapsed body.

A judgemental character appears from the wings. 'That person needs an ambulance.' The ambulance quickly arrives. They pull Michael out from under the desk. He is petrified in a mangled shape, like a squished bug that's been dried out in the sun. It is very hard for them to fit him in the back of the van with his limbs bent and stiff and contorted at every angle. Only then does it dawn on me that I should have helped him earlier, and that when he needed help I kicked him under the desk and kept working.

'That's me!' my mother says. 'That's what I always did! I kept working . . .'

★

My sister Rachel, who lives with her mother a mile away, comes over for dinner but she doesn't want to look through all the things I found in the desk. I tell her that maybe we don't need to be afraid of the past and all the skeletons falling out of drawers. Maybe if we all could just hold the things in our hands and really look at them – what seems frightening might reveal its other face, something much more ordinary. Our father's pain was much more ordinary and relatable than I had imagined.

'Yeah, OK. Maybe. Anyway . . .' she says because she has her own way of dealing with things. She chose to leave the chaos of our house at such a young age and she came back as a teenager and she has made her peace and doesn't need to drive herself crazy with pieces of paper to understand it. But then she does tell me a story I've never heard before. How one time Pandora the baby stole a lip balm from Boots when Rachel was pushing the pram. Later that night the police came around because my parents were arguing or something – Rachel doesn't remember exactly – but she thought they were there for the lip balm. She hid Pandora upstairs and then came downstairs to tell the police: 'But she's just a baby!'

★

Safe, safe, safe, the heart of the house beats soundly. My mother snores soundly and the furniture of our life breaks into a thousand indecipherable pieces in my head. Take the desk apart and put the desk back together. Make a mess, clean up the mess and outline it. Draw a line around it. Draw a wall around it, draw a window, open the window and let some air in. Stick your head out the window and lose it. Walk up the hill and lie down in a patch of bent grass where a cow once lay down. How do you let go? How do you stop being so afraid of cows? How do you become one with the cows? How do you go home with all the cows? The grass is grey. You had joy in your pocket and then you lost your pocket. It's really exhausting living but if you don't try then you will only want to lie down.

★

Have two baths. Look up skin crawling, creepy-crawlies. Look up mental illness relating to feeling objects under the skin. Feel brain squeaking inside skull. Feel the wind in the leaves, breathe the leaves, become green, become door. No no no. Become stairs. No! Become get back into bed and close eyes and be by the window because it's bed season. The room is so still. Woolf says, Stop sloshing around in your own emotions! Open the window. Peel off the pane. Snap the pain into pieces. Love absolutely. Smile at the flies absolutely.

A box of flowers comes through the door. Words on the box read: *We don't just send flowers. We care wildly.* So care wildly! Care wilder than the marketing on a cardboard box of delivered flowers. Do not love in a box if you can help it. Break your heart and put it together again. Love everyone who is around to be loved. Let all the splintered parts of you join all the splintered parts of everything else and then put all the splinters inside something so you don't go totally insane. Draw a vase around it. Draw any shape around it. It can be clumsy and wonky so long as it holds the pieces!

★

'I'm giving away Dad's desk,' I tell Pandora on the phone.
    'Why would you do that? That's his special desk.'
    'Me and Mum think it has bad vibes.'
    'No. I'll have it. Put it in my room. Don't get rid of the desk, Helen.'
    'OK.'
    'Don't, Helen. Don't get rid of it.'
    'I won't!' I say.

★

Light a candle in Dad's empty office. Put down a yoga mat. Call it a zen room. Call it a room for Mum to do exercise in. Open the window. The only problem is the new smell of dead rat. Don't search for a smell in a room with nothing in it. Breathe in, breathe out, breathe rat. Move Pandora's old desk up the stairs in pieces. You can change your life in pieces. Call the room your office. It's my office now, sorry Mum. Move the desk next to the window, move the desk away from the window. Sit on the floor beside the cigarette burns in the carpet and a pile of the remaining political science books. *The Relentless Revolution. Global Political Economy. Poverty and Progress. New Economic Order.* No wonder he was depressed. Addiction and depression is a rational response to an irrational system. That's where he died, just there. That's where the cigarette fell and he almost burned the house down. Put the plates in the dishwasher, invite Rachel over for dinner, hear the birds in the evening, listen to the sheep, listen to your mother. Move the desk, don't move the desk. Every time Mum comes upstairs the rooms are in a new arrangement. She says it looks wonderful. She says you have a real knack for this, unlike her. Tell her the desk is still wrong. The window is wrong. The carpet is wrong. Tell her your life is wrong. You did all the wrong things. You keep doing all the wrong things. The walls smell like dead rat and you are so lonely you are about to fall off the edge of the room! She will make a nice dinner. She will put on some calming music, she will eat from her plate with the spotlight shining and she will say that your dad was the one who taught her how to make a home. She will say if the desk is wrong it means that whatever you're working on is worthwhile. She will say that writing is betrayal. That making a family is dangerous. That as you get older, life gets richer, but it's richer from all the layers of love and sadness and loss. Tell her that all may be so but there is definitely a dead rat somewhere in the walls of that room.

'How do you have a conversation with a ghost?' she asks.

'What?' I say, thinking, Oh no. I have made her crazy now too.

'Open the walls so you can talk to him.'

'Huh?'

'Open up the heart!'

★

. . . suffering, remorse, abandonment of responsibility, thoughts of death, the peace of the grave, self-flagellation, suffering, remorse, abandonment of responsibility, thoughts of death, the peace of the grave, self-flagellation, suffering, remorse, abandonment of responsibility, thoughts of death, the peace of the grave, self-flagellation, suffering, remorse, abandonment of responsibility, thoughts of death, the peace of the grave, self-flagellation, suffering, remorse, abandonment of responsibility, thoughts of death, the peace of the grave, self-flagellation, suffering, remorse, abandonment of responsibility, thoughts of death, the peace of the grave, self-flagellation . . . It lives in the walls. It sinks through the floorboards. It drips on

the lamps. It turns saxophones into violins. It comes up the stairs to find me and it smells like dead rat!

★

Change the bed around, change the room around. Change your life. Get a job. Get out of the house. Move away, run away, wash up on a strange shore and the room is the same. It will always be the same room. All our fumbling human folly. The same problems in a new arrangement. Open a window. Stay close to the window and look out on to a wide world, God's green garden, where the wind blows and the grass grows with the pulse of the heart and the pulse of the spirit. There's harmony in a new arrangement. There is a song to be found inside every new, miraculous day. A new arrangement and you can't imagine how you ever lived differently. We have to keep moving forward. We have to keep moving something. *Do not move stones*, Sappho says in the book that is still by the toilet. But we shouldn't be stones either. We have to be moved. We have to.

★

Is it worth it? Someone asks inside my head. Sitting by the window all day. All this time and space? Is it worth being alive today? My answer today is . . . yes! At the top of the hill the leaves sounded like the ocean. The birds looked like fish in the sky. One must have swum through my inner organs. The trees were letting go of leaves so easily as if the wind was just water flowing. A spider hovers in the windowpane and makes shadows on the page. A fly pounces around by the lamp. The fly is my friend today. Reminds me of Michael on a good day for some reason. A day when he was not buzzing, criticising in my ear, but sitting, musing, crouching in the long grass, feeling the world, feeling life, paying attention.

★

'Some people are anti-narrative,' my mother says. 'But that's not how I work. I need narrative. I survive by finding a narrative in anything. I could make up a narrative about this spoon. But you are not making a narrative out of a spoon, you are just stuck with the spoon. What you need to do now is find a way to put the spoon down and just move on . . .'

★

The kitchen is blocking up a well. Drops of ceiling fall in my tea. The spring is in the cupboards. The cupboards smell like rank river. The slugs come in at night and my mother hasn't cried in ten years. Waterlogged spring. Will a wall collapse? She's worried that when her ten-year blockage bursts she will be flooded. I worry that I will be crying for ever. I worry about the kitchen and get in and out of there as quick as I can. There are puddles on the floor every morning. Ceiling drips on my hair when I'm doing the dishes. Maybe I should take the pots out of the cupboard and find the problem. But I'm fatigued from pointlessly moving furniture and mixing things up because I can't sit still. Won't the well just burst and take this doomed kitchen out the front door? I don't know but Emma calls. She says, 'Are you OK? You sound strange.' I say I think I'm mentally ill again. She says, 'Me too.' She says, 'Come to Chicago, come stay with us! There's no leaks here, just a bunk bed with your name on it. And Max has a new tic where he has to touch the wall of every room four times before he can leave it.'

★

At a pretentious coffee shop in the city centre, my mother is telling me about an Eliane Elias song that she and my father loved. A cover of a Bill Evans piece. Actually not a cover, she explains. The song begins with a scratchy tape of Bill playing the piano maniacally, pounding and screaming, just going totally insane. And then at the end, she says, Eliane Elias joins him on the piano in her own recording. She finds the melody and then the scratchy tape ends and it's just the sound of her playing so beautifully, calming him down. My mother's eyes water slightly and her face crumples as she says this. She hasn't cried in ten years! It's like Eliane Elias has come into the cafe too. I can feel her hands fluttering on my shoulders. My mother touches both eyes with two fingers. 'It's wet!' she says.

★

My mother finally finds the song and plays it for me one afternoon. 'Introduction to "Here's Something for You"', it's called. She's in her office. I sit in a sunny patch on the sofa by the record player, looking at the jazz poster and all my dad's records and CDs while Bill Evans goes mad out of his head on the piano.

He's screaming and banging round and you can just about make out something beautiful underneath. A muffled scream again and it's just like those yells in the night that my dad would make when he was drunk out of his head or coming down from the drink. Madness as the piano pounds, Bill is laughing now. All over the house, throwing up the melody of a head spinning out and seeing where his fingers land and just when he is about to blow his head and take us with him . . . Eliane Elias comes in, just as my mother said she would. She teases out the melody that had been under the madness, she puts his hand on his chest and calms his raging heart, cool water, a breeze, a song, singing: 'Here's something for you . . .' And behind me sat in her armchair in her office by the window that looks out on to the path my mum is sobbing now. She holds her little head in her hands.

★

7 August 1997

Well, a pretty bad day yesterday. I drank – the day was mainly a write-off. It was noticed when I came home – Maureen was extremely upset. Matthew got involved – I went to bed feeling like shit. One week after we go through one crisis we end up in another, just as life at home had begun to settle down.

The impulse in the last few days has been this overwhelming fear and terror. In turning to the bottle I am aware that this is just going to lead to more trouble and fear. Ultimately it will lead to the breakdown of my relationship which is what I most value in this world. Why can't I keep that uppermost in my mind? If only I can do that I can get through the worst. If I fail at this I will be in big trouble – and worse than at present. I really need to make this commitment in my head again and stick to it. I made eight weeks and it's possible again. It is the early weeks that are hard and I can get through these.

The other thing is to find ways of dealing with the fears and of getting myself more positive about the tasks ahead and getting something done each day. Only then will I get the confidence back to be able to do the jobs I need to do and get out from under my present cloud. I was doing well before. I can get back up to it again. I am feeling pretty demoralised this morning, under the cloud of the loss of Maureen's trust and generally being distant and fed up – she could hardly sleep last night either. I took three pills in the end which has left me groggy this morning and flat. I need to get some work done today and hopefully that will help. I am really headed for trouble if I don't pull myself together. If I can stick to my promise and keep from drinking at least I won't have trouble on the home front.

The whole year has been ruled by relapse after relapse. Really after the first one I lost a lot of confidence in myself and the belief in the program and what I can do for myself. I need to believe that I can make it, that this is really important, that the alternative is disaster on every front, and not turn to the bottle at every moment of hurt and pain and self-doubt. If I don't pull this to the front of my mind every day I will be fucked – how to keep the consequence in the front of my mind, that is the hard part. I need to have this beaten into my mind on a daily basis. I must do this, it is all that is possible for me and I must channel the anxiety and fears in other directions – work on that aspect as well so that life does not get out of hand again. I have a good life at least at home despite its tensions, its problems, the endless headaches and so on – it is all I have and to lose everything would put me in a position of despair.

Some in AA say you have to lose everything but in my view that is a self-justification for those that have. I have to prove to myself that it is possible to recover without going that far, but that does mean taking steps on a daily basis and really, really convincing myself that I have to sustain abstinence or my life will go down the tubes. It is a matter of life and death for me but I have to put that in the front of my mind today and every day. I will not drink today — there is no excuse.

★

The flies have died, just as my mother said they would. I swept them all up and now it is the autumn of the moths. Tiny moths that sleep on the walls and flutter every so often to remind me that I live in an eternal bughouse with walls that are part of a land that is alive and ready to move or drive me crazy at any instant. I pull a small, old book from the shelf of my father's books, to hit one that is annoying me. But the book is called *The Luminous Trail*, by Rufus M. Jones. It is a Quaker mystic's enquiry into the spirit of Jesus Christ, made luminous by the lives and work of saintly men and women over the centuries, and that is not an appropriate thing to kill a moth with. Flicking through the pages, Jones writes of the Eternal Yes, Infinite Love and the inner light of God that lives inside all of us, even those who have yet to know it. *There is in most of us a vast acreage of our inner estate which has never been touched by the plow* . . . I believe him and am ready to be taken, but skip all the way to the last page anyway, where the book ends with a passage about his saintly son, who died at the age of eleven and a memory of loss that reads like a vision:

When my sorrow was at its most acute stage I was walking along a great city highway . . . I saw a little child come out of a great gate, which swung to and fastened behind her. She wanted to go to her home behind the gate but it would not open. She pounded in vain with her little fist. She rattled the gate, then she wailed as though her heart would break. The cry brought the mother. She caught the child in her arms and kissed away the tears. 'Didn't you know I would come? It is all right now.' All of a sudden I saw with my spirit that there was love behind my shut gate.

Yes, 'where there is so much love, there must be more.'

★

'Come on, Helen, give me a break. The house is nice now! Allister did all this work on it. It doesn't smell. It's just the damp. It's just an old house. But it's beautiful. People always say it's a beautiful house. It's been my haven.'

'Sorry, I know. It's not just the house. It's my head. My head gets under my skin. It's just the way I experience it.'

'It's OK, darling,' she says. 'You can be cruel but you're cruel with heart.'

★

Oh my god, my father broke our hearts but he adored us. Walled-up, leaking person that he was. The walls are crumbling in this old house he bought from the crystal thrower with a pet pig. My mother says the walls are not crumbling and the house is fine. We could be taken under but we are held by something. She is cooking downstairs and the water flows down the walls and under her feet. Music travels up the stairs, with the sound of chopping herbs, onions and pots and pans in the infinite space between things. Because heartbreak is not so bad. But a walled-up heart . . . why stay suffering?

Acknowledgements

This book has taken so many years and so many people and homes opened up and hearts opened up and garbage drafts and conversations and meltdowns and hot meals placed on the table in front of me when I'd forgotten to eat. At the end of the day, it is just a book and a first attempt at something. At the same time it has been cobbled and held together by hundreds and the same goes for myself. To quote my sister Emma . . . 'Yeah, you have a lot of people to thank.'

I want to thank Tracy Bohan, who understood what I was trying to do before I did. With her kindness, intuition and constant encouragement, she's made the entire thing possible. She is, quite simply, the best agent anyone could hope for.

I'm so grateful to the team at Jonathan Cape and to my editor Hannah Westland, for her immeasurable insight and patient belief in pushing the work to be more than I could imagine alone. And thank you too, Luke Brown, for seeing the book that wasn't quite there yet and helping to make it whole. Thank you to Sarah-Jane Forder for her final expert assistance.

Parts of this book were first published in a slightly different form. Thank you to Valerie Steiker at the *New Yorker* and to Sophie Haigney and Emily Stokes at the *Paris Review* for their insightful questions and brilliant edits.

I want to thank my MA class at Goldsmiths, University of London and my teachers Blake Morrison and Ardashir Vakil, under whose wise supervision I wrote the first versions of many parts of this book. I'm also very grateful for the support and writing wisdom from Thomas Morris during his *Stinging Fly* workshop and beyond.

Thank you to Art Omi and the April 2022 cohort for such a cheerful and studious month in Upstate New York. Thanks to Felipe for his astute edits.

It takes courage to write, but it takes a whole other kind of courage to be written about. I am deeply grateful to everyone whose names and lives fall across these pages. Special thanks to my oldest, long-suffering friends – Abigail, Sally, Yasameen, Theo and George – who have not only let me include them but who have read so many drafts and been so encouraging over the years, especially in the hardest times when it mattered the most. Thank you to Kip and Grace just because you absolutely deserve a mention here too. Thank you to my second parents, Sally, Geoffrey and Aunty Eileen. And thank you to Gina, Fernanda, Laura, Dizz and Melissa, whose friendship, generosity and creativity have been instrumental. They've inspired the work in so many ways that

I've lost track. Thanks to Henry for his encouragement throughout a lost year. Thanks to Thom, Sez, Joana and the rest of the team at Peckham Cellars for creating such a cheerful, strange and inspiring place to work in the final stages. And thanks to Sinéad, Millie and Flora for the cosy London rest stop.

I am profoundly indebted to the housing department at the University of California, Santa Cruz, for assigning Rebecca as my room-mate. She was the missing piece. Eternal thanks to Rebecca for lighting up my life with her brilliance and strangeness. Thank you to Jack for reminding me to keep my chin up and my pencil sharp and also for letting me keep the part about his dirty floor (which has much improved). And thank you to Pero for allowing me to write about such a hard time in his life, from which now he has come so far. Thank you to Michael for living the story and deepest thanks to his family, Gene, Linda, Bonnie and Paul, for the love and the music.

I'm more grateful than I can say to my siblings, for giving my version of our family story their blessing and unwavering support, and for raising me too. So thank you Matthew, Kimber, Emma, Rachel, Pandora and my wonderful in-laws, Cash, Özge and Camy, and the niblings too. Double thanks to my sisters Emma and Pandora for reading everything I've ever written and taking such good care of me along the way. Thanks to Paul for his enthusiasm and wise advice. And thank you to my nephew Max for giving this book its best lines.

I want to thank my dad, Frank, who never got a say in this but who I hope would find in these pages a testament to who he was and how he struggled and what he gave as a father. I should also thank him for writing his Life Story on ten sheets of paper, and leaving it in a box for me to find at the very end, confirming all the stories my mum had already told me. I thank his stepsisters Elizabeth and Tori and their families for giving me a home away from home. And I thank my Aunt Lucy, for giving me her brutally honest depiction of addiction before she passed.

There is too much to thank my mother for. She's the beating heart of this book which is why I dedicate it to her. In her life and work she has inspired and taken in so many writers and students and lost souls, of which I am just one. She has taught me to take my work seriously, but most importantly, to live.

Thanks finally to the writers and musicians, living and dead, who have kept me company in the process and taught me to understand memory as a channel to the larger things beyond words. And thanks to Matt who understands this the most and has given me more than I can say.

To reference Jean Rhys one last time, the dream is to write of light, not glare. Because a single story of a single family is never just about itself. There are things in every room we share.

About the Author

Helen Longstreth is a writer currently based in the UK. She has been published in the *New Yorker* and *Paris Review*. *Things in Every Room* is her debut book, and she is currently working on her first novel.